Wilderness 101

Wilderness 101

KNOWLEDGE, SKILLS, AND FUNDAMENTALS FOR EVERY ADVENTURER

Maurice L. Phipps

ESSEX, CONNECTICUT

FALCONGUIDES®

An imprint of Globe Pequot, the trade division of The Rowman & Littlefield Publishing Group, Inc.
4501 Forbes Blvd., Ste. 200
Lanham, MD 20706
www.rowman.com

Falcon and FalconGuides are registered trademarks and Make Adventure Your Story is a trademark of The Rowman & Littlefield Publishing Group, Inc.

Distributed by NATIONAL BOOK NETWORK

Copyright © 2022 by Maurice L. Phipps
Illustrations by Fred Schmidt unless otherwise noted

British Library Cataloguing in Publication Information available

Library of Congress Cataloging-in-Publication Data Available

ISBN 9781493065028 (pbk. : alk. paper) | ISBN 9781493065035 (epub)

∞™ The paper used in this publication meets the minimum requirements of American National Standard for Information Sciences—Permanence of Paper for Printed Library Materials, ANSI/NISO Z39.48-1992.

Contents

Preface

In 1962, while heading up the southern slope of Ben Nevis, the sky was clear, and there was snow on the ground, so we were kicking steps as we neared the top. There were three of us youngsters with two ice axes and a stick. The views from the top were stupendous to us kids from Derbyshire (which has nice but less spectacular views). We were "in the moment" all the way up there but didn't know a lot of what we should have known.

We were an ice axe short, which became a problem at one snowfield, but, after some discussion, we found a way around it. We didn't have any training in using the axes, so they probably wouldn't have helped us if we had fallen anyway. We didn't have crampons for our boots. We knew we had to climb with care—two days before, when we arrived at Steall Hut in Glenn Nevis, someone had given us his spare food, as his wife had fallen, and that was the end of their trip. We were 16 years old and considered ourselves somewhat invincible and so were not deterred. We were lucky with the weather, as it can turn into Arctic conditions in no time. I discovered that firsthand four years later when I returned as a college student—that time with a guide—and conditions were so bad that we opted to kayak near Mallaig instead.

So we were lucky to not have had to experiment trying to stop a fall with our stick and two ice axes, and we were also lucky that we didn't have to battle any ferocious weather, which could easily have happened. Maybe we would have stayed in the hut, but we could have been caught out if the weather had changed while we were out during the day. We also knew nothing about hypothermia. When I went again later on my college trip, we did stop in the middle of a snowstorm to make a cup of tea! We did eventually make it home from both trips, and the atrocious weather on my college trip even made it a bit more exciting. Since no one got hurt on either trip, we were all eager for more. We were lucky both times, though. Even the kayaking from Arisaig to Mallaig could have been a disaster if anyone had capsized in the canvas kayaks we were paddling, as we had no rescue training, and the sea temperature in April would have given us hypothermia in minutes. So we lucked out. But many people aren't so lucky. We all need to know what we don't know about venturing out into the wild outdoors, or else we could possibly suffer dire consequences.

Since my early days of outdoor adventuring, I have gone through training with the British Canoe Union, the Australian Canoe Federation, and the Wilderness Education Association. I have worked at mountain outdoor pursuits centers, started a private outdoor school in the United Kingdom and the Mitta Mitta Canoe Club in Australia, worked for the Wilderness Education Association in the United States, and taught in universities for more than 30 years. I have both attended and taught courses in different countries and experienced outdoor activities in the United Kingdom, North America, Australia, New Zealand, Europe, Central America, and the Caribbean.

My research in universities included different aspects of outdoor activities, including leadership, group dynamics, outdoor instruction, energy use in climbing, and snow and ice axe techniques. My teaching in universities included one- to five-week expedition courses in the Tetons, the Wind River Range, Colorado, upstate New York, Yellowstone (winter and summer), Texas, and North Carolina.

One of the university courses I taught for many years focused on how to avoid the need for survival techniques when heading into the backcountry. I learned much from the legendary mountaineer Paul Petzoldt when I apprenticed with him on his last Teton Wilderness Education Association course and then cotaught expedition courses with him. One of his tenets was the idea of avoiding survival situations. The course that I taught on this subject was rooted in his beliefs and was very popular with students. This was the impetus to write this book and enable people to go into the wild outdoors with more knowledge than I did or when Paul did when he climbed the much more technical Grand Teton when he was 16. The idea of this book is to show the reader what you don't know, or, as Paul used to often say, "Know what you know and know what you don't know."

Introduction

So you want to do something adventurous? Maybe you've seen hair-raising videos online, or perhaps you aren't ready for that level of activity but would like to experience the outdoors, such as by hiking in the woods or paddling on a lake. What do you know about any of this? If you are a beginner, you probably know enough to be dangerous and possibly get into some kind of predicament that then requires survival techniques.

There are many things the average person has no idea about, such as hiking over moats (snow-covered rivers or waterfalls).

This book is about learning what you don't know to avoid getting into a survival situation. There are some things that are common sense but still entice people to dangerous situations, such as visiting waterfalls. There are many things the average person has no idea about, such as hiking over moats (snow-covered rivers or waterfalls), which could result in a very quick death, or hiking in wet and moderately cold temperatures wearing cotton, which could result in a slower death through hypothermia. Let's look at some examples.

Many people each year decide to explore the waterfalls of North Carolina. Some like to view them from below, and then there are others who head for the view from the top. The top has swift water, leaves, and slick rock, so the odds of these folks having a serious fall have increased dramatically, including that some of these people will fall to the bottom, which could mean death or serious injury. One of North Carolina's waterfalls, Paradise Falls, required two Black Hawk helicopter rescues in only one two-week period in 2017.

An incident at another waterfall, Glen Falls, illustrates the consequences. A 21-year-old woman was hiking with friends at Glen Falls two miles outside of Highlands when she slipped and fell about 80 feet. She was airlifted to a local hospital where she was treated for her injuries, which were reportedly "a crushed ankle, a collapsed lung, a broken jawbone and teeth, broken bones in her back and deep cuts to her groin and head from the fall." Her fall was the second at Glen Falls in one month. A 16-year-old boy was injured after falling at the same spot on June 16.[1]

Several groups in the past have decided to descend a gulley on Symmetry Spire in the Grand Tetons mountain range in Wyoming. Some of these groups were not seasoned mountaineers and didn't know what they didn't know about the risk of there being waterfalls or moats under the snow. Two incidents illustrate this:

Incident 1
The trio was descending the couloir (gulley) and glissaded (slid) into a deep moat at the bottom of a cliff.

There they were trapped by snow falling in around them. The snow also dammed the stream that ran beneath the snow surface, filling the moat with icy water.[2]

Incident 2

Their descent route was channeled into a narrow snow chute that ended in a 60-foot waterfall and moat. One member of the group saw the moat and was able to grab some bushes and stop himself but was unable to hold onto a second member who slid over the falls into the moat. The first member yelled to a third member, and at the last moment, he was able to vault the moat and land downslope from the falls. The first member then grabbed the fourth member and was able to hold onto him. The second member was later found at the bottom of the waterfall, about 50 feet into the moat. He was lying facedown in about six inches of water with massive head injuries, showing no signs of life.[3]

Many years ago, I personally witnessed a body recovery from Spalding Falls in Wyoming: the victim had descended the snowfield after climbing the Grand Teton—but without an ice axe. Ice under the snow on the steep drop immediately above the falls resulted in a slide, so the climber dropped into a crevasse and the waterfall under the snow. He was unable to stop because he had no ice axe to use as a brake to prevent the slide. He was also likely unaware of the moat given that it was covered on the journey in. This accident was precipitated by two unknowns: knowledge of hidden moats and the need to have and be able to use an ice axe when traveling on snow in the mountains.

What about something seemingly minor, such as going hiking in jeans and a cotton flannel jacket in wet and cool weather? This is called an environmental hazard—in this case, hypothermia—which can strike anywhere there are cool, wet, and especially windy conditions.

A common saying among outdoor enthusiasts is "cotton kills."

When the body's temperature drops below 95°F (35°C) and is not brought back up to about 98°F (36.6°C), the result is hypothermia. That is a drop of only 3°F. Wearing cotton, which soaks up water efficiently, will cool down the body compared to wearing man-made fibers, such as fleeces or good old-fashioned wool. For this reason, a common saying among outdoor enthusiasts is "cotton kills." An example from the Adirondacks during a November hiking trip follows where the hikers had otherwise good gear but still chose to wear cotton. Despite having a new complement of "outdoorsy gear," two hikers were clad in all cotton. After getting waterlogged in an overly ambitious pursuit, an exhausted hiker with soaked cotton clothing succumbed to a hypothermic death before help could arrive.[4]

The previously mentioned examples show the need to be able to realize what you do know about yourself and an environment (i.e., knowing your limitations) and that there are things to learn before you venture out—things that you don't know (and need to learn). In other words, know what you know and know what you don't know.

Who coined the phrase "know what you know and know what you don't know"? We don't know for sure, but the legendary mountaineer Paul Petzoldt sure used it a lot. He also used to always say he wanted to live to be an old mountaineer by assessing the "Las Vegas odds" of whatever you were deciding to do. To illustrate what that means, he would bring in the historical figure Nick the Greek, a famed gambler, to make his point by saying, "Where would Nick the Greek bet we would have accidents when climbing today?" Petzoldt was a believer in avoiding survival situations by using good preparation before going rather than concentrating on survival techniques to help survive after getting into a predicament.[5] He developed what he called "control plans" to help in both the advance preparation and also during an activity. These included plans for health, time, energy, and climate control, which will be detailed in chapter 6.

MUST-KNOWS

So what kinds of things should a person wishing to venture into the wild outdoors know about? The following is a list of "must-knows":

1. Motivations for Going into the Wild Outdoors
Phrases such as "hold my beer" or "adrenaline is my drug" show the effects of alcohol or bravado when

trying to impress companions. These often override common sense. There are also unconscious motivations that drive us to do high-risk activities, especially for extreme adventure sports.

2. Terrain and Equipment

Where will you be going (e.g., whether there will be mountains, caves, forests, deserts, rivers, lakes, the sea, surf, gorges, and so on)? What equipment is needed to live and travel in the type of terrain that you choose?

3. Climate, Weather, Clothing, and Energy

Will where you're going be cold, warm, or hot? What are the expected problems related to the climate you are visiting, such as storms, rain, and snow? What clothing is suitable for the activity and the climate? To combat environmental injuries, you need energy, so are you carrying enough food and water, and are you stopping frequently to "gas up"? Your "gas tank" is for energy to move and energy to stay warm.

4. Problem Wildlife

How do you avoid problems with the local flora and fauna?

5. Skills for Hazards and Emergency Procedures

What specific skills are needed to accomplish your goals, such as hiking, camping, cooking, navigating, canoeing, kayaking, climbing, belaying, rappelling, climbing, caving, skiing, snowshoeing, sailing, self-rescuing, and using rescue and first-response techniques?

6. Control Plans

What control plans do you need to enable safer and more comfortable experiences in the wild outdoors?

7. Protecting the Environment
How do you engage in this activity while still protecting people and the environment?
8. Where to Go from Here
After reading this book, what should you do as you venture forth into the wild outdoors? Where can you find good instruction and courses to learn experientially?

This book provides examples of these must-knows, examples of accidents resulting from ignorance, and ways to avoid accidents and survival situations. Details will also be given on Petzoldt's control plans. This essential background will help the reader understand their own limitations. As Petzoldt used to say, "Know what you know and know what you don't know" before you venture into the wild outdoors and use good judgment in your decision making.

JUDGMENT
Judgment is the critical factor in reducing the chances of an incident or accident. Judgment surely comes from experience—right?

The brains trust   The reality

So how can you start acquiring good judgment as a beginner? Reading can help (but only a little). The best teacher is actual experience under the guidance of an instructor or a capable mentor. Progressions in the level of difficulty of activities should be made in small steps to lower the Las Vegas odds of mishaps. Many organizations offer courses in outdoor activities. Instruction is often done in groups, but individual instruction is also possible. Your guide or instructor needs to be qualified, so do some research on that before you sign up for a course. There are national qualifications in most outdoor activities, outdoor leadership, swift water rescue, and wilderness medicine, so check your potential instructor's qualifications and certifications.

Thus, judgment can be learned. After a lot of experience, the knowledge gained becomes tacit, and you don't have to go through the steps of decision making each time, as you have performed certain tasks so many times that you can simply do them. However, when situations change—as they do in the outdoors—judgment is needed as to what to do. Should you carry on, turn back, or modify the trip? The environment is fluid; for example, more rain increases the size and difficulty of the river when paddling, or the weather turns cold, making camping in winter a different kind of activity than it is in summer. The group you are in is also fluid, as different personalities also affect judgment in decision making. Thus, what is tacit knowledge on one day can turn into something different on another day with different people and in a different context.

Laurence Gonzales, in his book *Deep Survival*, suggests that judgment is also affected by emotion: "The knowledge involved in the risk-reward loop does not involve reasoning. It comes to the child coded in feelings, which represent emotional experiences in a particular environment."[6] He is saying that emotional reactions can affect logic adversely and that different environments or subtly different hazards can result in inappropriate actions and reactions for all of us because of unconscious memories of feelings. An example is running a drop in a canoe, something that produces a feeling of exhilaration that one might want to repeat. Staying focused by being in the present and updating your assessment of a situation as factors change will help with these judgment factors and thought processes where emotional reactions might override logic. Another key issue is being aware of time—how long does it actually take to do things?

BE HERE AND NOW

Gonzales came up with two "Rules of Life" with his daughter when she was six years old about survival and the avoidance of survival situations:

1. Be here now (pay attention to keeping your "mental model" current; i.e., being present and updating your assessment of the situation as factors change).
2. Everything will take eight times as long as you expect.

The idea of item 1 is to stay attuned to where you are and what is happening and not to become a "sheep" if you are in a group. Instead, you need to stay tuned into what is going on all the time regardless of whether you are the group leader or not. Sheep mentality often comes into play during navigation practice. One person might take the lead with or without a map and the rest of the group follows along, oblivious to where they are going or to their surroundings.

For example, I know of an athletic director of a university in the southern Appalachians who was with his wife and two friends when they ended up spending the night in the woods, huddled together after following the person that "knew the way" to a waterfall. Many of the trails in that area are intersected by old logging roads, so after a couple of wrong turns and without a map and compass or a GPS unit, they were in for an uncomfortable and anxious night. They eventually found some students camping after following an old logging road the following morning, much to their relief. It has been common in my wilderness education classes for students to "not be here now" as well, so practicing without instructors being present is important. And they frequently did get lost. Getting lost even once encouraged them to be more in the here and now moving forward. Of course, Gonzales is talking about more than navigation—he is talking about all situations in life, be it driving, hiking, climbing, or whatever activity you are doing.

For item 2 in the list above, it is common for things to take longer than you think they will. For example, how long does it take you to walk a mile? Now consider it on the track, on a trail, on a trail with elevation, off a trail, and off a trail with elevation. This could also include heavy bush pushing (the term for bushwhacking without using machetes), snow and ice, and different kinds of weather. So we need to also include energy in how far you plan to travel and how long it will take considering the abilities of the person involved. It could take you anywhere from 15 minutes to hours, depending on the terrain and weather.

When you're with a group, things take much longer, as each individual has to deal with, for example, heel problems, backpack problems, different levels of strength, navigation problems, and so on. Larger groups, say, of 10 beginners, sometimes travel at only one mile per hour on the trail. Understanding how long things take—such as cooking a meal or rigging food bag hangs before it gets dark or packing to move camp and getting to another site early enough before snow softens—can reduce survival situations.

For example, with a group of 10 beginners, it can take four hours to cook breakfast, go to the toilet, take down tents, and pack backpacks. This time can be reduced to less than half with experienced back-packers, but where are you and your group on the experience continuum? What if there is a river that needs to be crossed using a Tyrolean traverse? With a practiced group, it could easily take four hours. Estimating time accurately becomes a critical piece in avoiding survival situations.

TYROLEAN TRAVERSE

The chance of mishaps occurring in the wild out-doors is great, but this can be tempered by using good judgment about where you are going, who you are going with, whether you go on a course, or whether you hire an instructor or guide. Look at the Las Vegas odds of possible accidents for whatever you are doing. Before taking that first step, ask yourself, "What are the potential consequences?"

Remember that any evacuation could be both very long and very painful.

All this depends on your knowing your limitations and knowing what you know and what you don't know. Remember also that any evacuation could be both very long and very painful. It could also be very expensive.

To encapsulate, the four things to remember to help keep you safe are the following:

1. Use good judgment—from Petzoldt.
2. Be here now—from Gonzales.
3. Everything takes a lot longer than you think—from Gonzales.
4. Look at the Las Vegas odds of bad consequences—from Petzoldt.
5. Know what you know and know what you don't know—from Petzoldt.

The focus of this book is to illustrate what you need to know and to help you know what you don't know about the wild outdoors. Judgments and control plans will be given to help you avoid getting into survival situations.

Motivations for Going into the Wild Outdoors

Motivations for going into the wild outdoors—phrases such as "hold my beer" or "I don't need drugs"—show the effects of bravado or alcohol when trying to impress companions. These often override common sense. There are also unconscious motivations that drive us to do high-risk activities, especially for extreme adventure sports.

"HOLD MY BEER"

Many times, people (often young men) do testosterone-driven things that result in injury or death. It is often done in front of a group or camera to show off. It often is preceded by the statement "hold my beer" before the person leaps of a cliff into the lake or some other death-defying activity.

Examples

- "Hold my beer and watch this!"

- "Hold my beer while I jump over this fire!"

- "Hold my beer while I jump off this cliff into the lake!"

- "Y'all, watch this!"

Consequences
The consequences are usually bad, as judgment has been suspended. These incidents often involve alcohol coupled with a wish to impress by doing something very risky.

THE SELFIE
A modern development on this theme that doesn't seem to be gender correlated is the "selfie," where people stand in front of wild animals, close to raging surf, or on the edge of cliffs or giant dams and trains to take the last picture they might ever take. Numerous deaths occur every year from this phenomenon. On a visit to Iceland, we noticed large warning billboards at most tourist areas, such as the Black Sand Beach and the edges of glaciers, that included pictorial illustrations of possible consequences from this behavior.

Examples
• Several people have drowned at Reynisfjara Black Sand Beach in Iceland because of "sneaker" waves that are larger than normal and sneak up on the unsuspecting person at the edge of the water. The water is cold even during the summer.

• Another Icelandic selfie problem is people standing on floating icebergs not realizing that, if they slip off, the water is very cold and that hypothermia would only be minutes away.

• In warmer Italy, a 16-year-old girl died in Taranto after plunging 60 feet onto rocks while taking a selfie at the seafront.

• A 21-year-old man from Yogyakarta, Indonesia, died after falling into the crater of Mount Merapi while attempting to take a selfie.

• A man was struck by lightning at Brecon Beacons in Wales while taking a selfie instead of heading downhill to safety.

• A 68-year-old Belgian woman stepped backward while taking a selfie into scalding water while visiting a geyser field in the Andes Mountains in South America.

• A 51-year-old German tourist did a "flying selfie" at Machu Pichu but fell 130 feet after losing his balance.

• A 66-year-old Italian tourist was trampled by an elephant in Kenya after trying to take a selfie with the elephant.

Wikipedia lists an additional 253 selfie-caused deaths between 2011 and 2017 besides the above examples. Many of these involve trains, but many involve incidents in the backcountry. It also seems that selfie-related deaths aren't age related—they're not happening only to young people.

Consequences

Usually, an untimely death is the consequence of the participant not being "in the moment" and thinking about safety or else actually doing something risky to impress with a picture that could be put on social media (see the "Hold My Beer" section at the beginning of the chapter).

JOINING 'THE LAST SELFIE CLUB'

ONE-WAY LOOKOUT POINTS

Another variation is where couples visit lookout points in parks and other scenic places and only one person comes back, perhaps because the outlook is on the edge of a cliff and, like in the examples in the "Selfie" section, they are not paying attention to being in a precarious position. Or it can be an individual simply falling over the edge.

Examples

• Woman falls to her death from Sunset Point on Lookout Mountain, Chattanooga

• Yosemite deaths: Couple fall from iconic photo spot at Taft Point

Consequences

Most often, falls such as these will lead to death or serious injury.

EXTREME SPORTS

Other developments have been the mushrooming popularity of extreme adventure pursuits, such as BASE jumping (jumping off a cliff, tower, or building to parachute to the ground), flying using wingsuits, free climbing (climbing without rope protection), kayaking down large waterfalls, or skiing down enormous drops.

The Las Vegas odds of accidents are "upped" considerably when doing extreme sports.

Examples

• Mountain boarding: Cross-country skateboarding

• Kiting: Using the wind and a board on snow, water, or sand

• Zorbing: Getting inside a giant ball and rolling downhill

- Parkour: Running and jumping between obstacles

- Hang gliding: Gliding using a frame covered by fabric

- Wingsuit flying: Flying with special suits and a parachute

- Waterfall kayaking: Running large waterfalls

- Extreme skiing or snowboarding: Snow sports that involve going over big drops

- Highlining: Slack lining done at high heights

- Free climbing or solo climbing: Climbing without ropes on long routes

- Canyon swinging: Pendulum swinging on a rope off a cliff

- Bungee jumping: Jumping off a structure with an elastic rope

- Cave diving: Exploring underwater caves using scuba equipment

Consequences

The Las Vegas odds of accidents are "upped" considerably when doing extreme sports. You also have to consider that you are in the wild outdoors, so rescue and evacuations are more difficult. As there is a higher degree of risk, there is more chance of death or injury.

MOTIVATIONS

So why do people do such things? There are many reasons, some obvious and some not so obvious. Two reasons could be immaturity and poor judgment. Current research indicates that the judgment functions of the brain do not develop fully until the age of 25.[1] If someone has seen exciting videos or wants to one-up their friends, then they may take the leap, so to speak. The ability to record the event on cell phones or GoPro cameras has increased the likelihood of this, as they can also post their "feat" on social media for a wider audience. This means there could be peer pressure from both the immediate group and peers on social media. The person involved may not be ready in their skill development if the action involves skill. Or it could be something such as leaping off a cliff into a lake where the perception is that a skill isn't needed but that there is still a high risk. Add in alcohol, and you have impaired

COURAGE IN A BOTTLE

judgment and impaired skill—hence the common saying "hold my beer" just before something stupid happens. However, other potential motivations are explored below.

I Don't Need Drugs—This Is My High

It may be an adrenaline rush that someone is after. When danger is perceived, the biochemistry of the brain changes with the release of adrenaline, dopamine, and endorphins. These chemicals affect your physiological responses to enable maximum responses to meet the danger and afterward give a feeling of well-being or sometimes a "high" from having "gotten away" with the challenge. My students often were unbelievably "pumped" after running the Nantahala Falls at the end of a kayak course in North Carolina. To say they were high in some cases was an understatement. Of course, not meeting the challenge might produce the opposite result if they end up spending a few months (or longer) recovering from an accident with a long time to think about it.

UNCONSCIOUS MOTIVATIONS

Let's look at some psychological reasons for why we go into the wild outdoors and push ourselves. As mentioned in this book's introduction, Laurence Gonzales suggested in his book *Deep Survival* that judgment is also affected by emotion and that these emotional reactions can adversely affect logic. Therefore, different environments or subtly different hazards can result in inappropriate actions and reactions

for all of us because of unconscious memories of feelings. Here he is talking about personal unconscious memories and feelings, such as the elation you felt when you went off your first ski jump and want to repeat with a bigger jump. This is reinforced until the jump is too big, you didn't weigh the Las Vegas odds, and now you are looking down at your broken leg.

The elation you feel when completing a climb, running a river rapid, or skiing the double black diamond run is what psychologist Abraham Maslow referred to as a *peak experience*, psychiatrist Carl Jung referred to as a *numinous experience*, and psychologist Mihaly Csikszentmihalyi referred to as a *flow* experience. During such an experience, one becomes so engrossed in the activity that one loses one's sense of time and space and often experiences a sense of euphoria. Like a drug, it can be addictive, so people may seek more such experiences at increasing difficulty levels. At some point, fear can overcome the motivation to increase the level of difficulty, such as launching into a class V rapid or dropping over a 20-foot waterfall. The point when this happens seems to vary for people, requiring differing amounts of brain stimulation to satisfy their need for a peak experience. What could a peak experience look like? The following is an example that uses mental imagery to illustrate what these experiences can be like. This example relates to running the Second Ledge rapid on the Chattooga River in the southeastern United States:

> Imagine you are on the Chattooga River in a boat. It is a bright and sunny day and the river is running at a comfortable level for you. The water is absolutely clear and you can see the rocks all the way to the bottom of the river and the "Fools' Gold" (mica) shining on the sandy riverbed. There is a strong smell of pine as the river pushes you down through the wilderness. You are approaching Second Ledge, slipping through the rocks just upstream and heading for river left. You can hear the waterfall. You did this run a couple of weeks ago and it is still fresh in your mind. You aim some yards off the left bank, but as there are some low hanging branches, you need to stay right enough to stay away from them. The sound is loud now, there is mist rising from the edge of the drop and no view of what is happening right below the horizon line. Your heart rate has picked up considerably. The boat in front disappears and you hope that you are positioned correctly now. As it is too late to change course, you power

through the next few strokes. You can see the edge
and you are on it in a nanosecond giving one last
pull to try and sail over the edge. You drop into the
hole and it's all froth and sparkling whitewater as
you pop to the surface, through the hydraulic, and
on downriver to join the other paddlers in the river-
right eddy under a giant rock.[2]

Want to repeat that? You bet. Want to up the
ante? This could depend on what that would entail.
Paddling farther down the river on section 4, the rapids are more difficult with serious consequences, as
failure on one rapid, such as Corkscrew, could result
in a swim through Crack in the Rock, a very dangerous rapid where several people running it have died.
Below Jawbone rapid is Hydroelectric Boulder, an
underwater tunnel that may have debris in it. Then
Sock-em-Dog rapid requires paddling hard off the
"Launching Pad" to jump the killer hydraulic under
it. This definitely ups the ante, and several people
have died doing this section, but it is very popular
among seasoned boaters. So nerve is needed, as is
skill. Simply having the nerve to do it without the
skill could be a disaster. The need for more excitement pushes folks to do more difficult things, but
fear can temper this need.

Age seems to also temper the need. I remember
kayaking the Oetztaler Ache in Austria when I was
25 years old. It was in flood and a continuous class
V river. The villagers came out to see the crazy Brits
putting in. We also knew that downriver was a killer
dam with a monster hydraulic. No problem, we

thought at first, except we ultimately lost two kayaks, and two participants quit the kayaking vacation the day after. The rest of us tried the River Inn in Switzerland the following day, which ended in a desperate rescue before we abandoned it to hike out. As of this writing, at the age of 75, even though I can still paddle advanced rivers, I know I wouldn't be going anywhere near these two rivers!

Seeking euphoria-inducing experiences can explain some people's motivation for engaging in these types of activities. But Carl Jung, the renowned Swiss psychiatrist, would say that there are others. Jung suggested that we have archetypes in our collective unconscious. The collective unconscious is the part of our unconscious that is shared by everyone, and it contains archetypes and instincts. We readily acknowledge instincts such as the fight, flight, and freeze responses. Archetypes are more complex and varied. An archetype is a predisposition to an image or a way of thinking. Three that are relevant to us here are the hero, the child, and the spirit. They are very powerful, and, as they are unconscious, we often don't know that they are what is driving us.

Let us consider the child archetype as a balance to the hero archetype.

First, let us consider the hero archetype, which should be familiar to us from movies, fairy tales, myths, and real life as we idolize film stars or sports celebrities, such as top skiers, kayakers, canoeists, cavers, and climbers. Think about why so many people want to climb Mount Everest, a brutal experience with significant odds of dying. If they make it, they can go to the local pub or post on social media to receive some kind of awe from the "regular" folks. This awe is a projection, and getting such projections from people can strengthen the ego, as it can make one feel good. However, doing an activity (it doesn't have to be climbing Mount Everest) simply for projections is a fool's errand, as eventually someone next to you at the bar in the pub is going to one-up you, and as you get older, they are definitely going to one-up you. There is the added danger that you may feel that you *are* the hero and "fly too close to the sun" like the mythical Icarus, whose wings made with wax melted, causing him to fall. For you, it could be a true fall from the cliff you were free-climbing. The hero archetype is a very powerful driver.

So let us consider the child archetype as a balance to the hero archetype to keep some kind of moderation. This way of looking at things would inspire you to do outdoor activities for fun and enjoyment rather than for projections from other people. This means that you don't have to do Everest or some other major Himalayan peak, drop down the Spiral Stairs ski run in Telluride, run Sock-em-Dog on the Chattooga River, or climb Cenotaph Corner in North Wales. You can play at a lower level simply for the fun and enjoyment.

The third important archetype that could help balance out the hero archetype is the spirit. Many people get spirituality from being in the wild outdoors as part of their personal growth. Jung's term for personal growth was "individuation." Roszak, in his book *The Voice of the Earth*, suggests that Jung's individuation may be the adventure of a lifetime, "but the person is anchored within a greater universal identity. . . . Salt remnants of the ancient oceans flow through our veins, ashes of expired stars rekindle in our genetic chemistry."[3] We are connected to the universe in this way and can become satisfied spiritually through our immersion into the wild outdoors in ways that can promote our personal growth.

CONCLUSION

While some motivations for going into the wild outdoors are obvious, some are not. It could be for pure excitement, fun, or spiritual reasons. It could also be for unconscious reasons, whether personal or driven by the archetypes from Jung's collective unconscious. For a more in-depth look at the unconscious motivations, consult this author's article "Adventure—An Inner Journey to the Self: The Psychology of Adventure Expressed in Jungian Terms," which has been reprinted in the book *Outdoor Instruction: Teaching and Learning Concepts for Outdoor Instructors.*[4]

It could be that you simply enjoy being in the wild outdoors or doing an activity with your friends out there, whether it be the wild outdoors itself, the bonding experience, or the joy of doing the activity itself. As Petzoldt said,

> All my life, people have asked the question, directly or indirectly, "Why in the hell do you climb

mountains?" I can't explain this to other people. I love the physical exertion. I love the wind. I love the storms. I love the fresh air. I love the companionship in the outdoors. I love the reality. I love the change. I love the rejuvenating spirit. I love to feel the oneness with nature. I'm hungry; I enjoy eating. I get thirsty; I enjoy the clear water. I enjoy being warm at night when it's cold outside. All those things are extremely enjoyable because, gosh, you're feeling them, you're living them, your senses are really feeling. I can't explain it.[5]

Remember:
1. Use good judgment.
2. Be here now.
3. Everything takes a lot longer than you think.
4. Look at the Las Vegas odds of bad consequences.
5. Know what you know and know what you don't know.

Terrain Skills
and Equipment

Where will you be going? Will there be mountains, caves, forests, deserts, rivers, lakes, seas, surf, gorges, and so on? What equipment is needed to live and travel in the type of terrain that you choose?

Doing serious research into where you are going is paramount. This is especially so today, as getting minimal information online is so easy and, hey, you will have your cell phone in case things go wrong, right? Not so fast.

Your cell phone may not work.

Your cell phone may not work because of poor reception or a dead battery. The minimal research that you did online didn't include map-reading skills that you thought you didn't need anyway because you have a GPS unit with you. Technology can give a false sense of security because when that GPS unit fails, you will need map and compass skills. As many wild areas are not yet "Google mapped" in detail, you need a map and compass anyway.

So in addition to doing research on the specific area where you are going, preparation includes learning navigation skills—yes, skills for using a GPS—but also good old-fashioned map and compass skills. It also includes the type of clothing and equipment that you need. But for any environment where you choose to go, there are specific hazards to know about, and these are described here.

MOUNTAINS
Must-Knows
Mountain areas have some obvious hazards, such as cliffs, rivers, ravines, and waterfalls, but also some less obvious hazards, such as moats (water flowing under snow); gullies (rock highways); rockfall at hotter times of the day; avalanche dangers after new snowfall; softer, deep snow in the afternoons (including stepping off rocks onto soft snow); crevasses (large

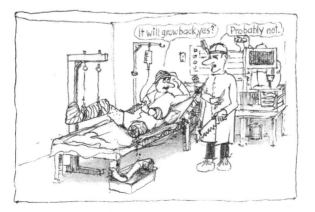

cracks in snow and ice); cornices (overhanging snow on ridges); scree slopes (small, loose stones forming a cover on a slope); boulder fields; verglas (clear ice) on rock and snow; altitude sickness problems; and, in some areas, problem animals, such as bears and mountain lions. There are significant temperature differences that require appropriate clothing to prevent hypothermia and frostbite.

Other weather factors include snowstorms that necessitate waiting in camp until avalanche dangers have passed. Early morning starts around 4:00 or even earlier are necessary to avoid afternoon storms that bring lightning.

Altitude problems often begin at about 7,000 feet. Altitude sickness symptoms can begin with tiredness and headaches. Progressing slowly to higher altitudes and sleeping at higher altitudes enables the body to adjust and acclimatize. The ability to adjust to altitude doesn't seem to necessarily correlate with fitness. Although fitness is important to mountaineering, it is not a protection against acute mountain sickness (AMS). AMS can affect judgment and induce hallucinations, and it can progress to high-altitude pulmonary edema (HAPE) and high-altitude cerebral edema (HACE). Many people die or become ill because they are unaware of or ignore that we are dependent on a sufficient amount of oxygen, which decreases with the increase in altitude. AMS is serious, and if symptoms do not quickly subside, then descent is necessary immediately. There are some medications that can be taken to assist the acclimatization process, but careful research on these medications is needed for each individual.

Skills and Equipment Needed

Associated climbing and camping equipment along with the skills to use it are needed. These skills include hiking, rock climbing, snow and ice climbing, rappelling, ice axe arrests, glacier travel, rock and crevasse rescue, navigation, and river-crossing skills. Camping skills include safe site selection and food protection skills. And, of course, there is always a possibility of injury, so add in wilderness first-aid skills. Many tools are available, such as ice axes, ropes, ice screws, ascenders, descenders, nuts, stoppers, chocks, camming devices, bolts, pitons, hammers, carabiners, harnesses, helmets, and, of course, camping gear and first-aid kits.

Clothing is often specialized (made with fleeces and man-made fibers) for shirts and pants, breathable

CLIMBING GEAR

overpants and overjackets, but beware of down in your sleeping bags or puffy jacket, as down works only when dry. Footwear is also specialized, with small, tight shoes for rock climbing but roomy leather boots for general mountaineering and plastic double boots for snow and glaciers. Gaiters are also needed to stop snow from getting into your boots. If you must take leather boots on snow, then impregnating the leather with silicone seems to do the best job in waterproofing them. Applying silicone spray is a useful way to ensure that any type of equipment will be waterproof (but not breathable).

FORESTS

Must-Knows

Forested areas make navigation more difficult, as features such as valleys, saddles, and ridges are less visible. Campsite selection includes being wary of dead trees (often called widow makers), being away from food hangs and camp kitchens, and keeping away from smells that attract wildlife. Traveling through forests on trails is very different from going off trail or bush pushing, which can be four or five times harder and can precipitate having to negotiate unseen cliffs. Patience and accuracy are needed to stay on course navigating off trail. It is rarely a shortcut. If you think you are lost, do you have a plan for that? If you are in a group and are unsure of where you are, you can send out "scouts" in pairs with strict instructions to return after half an hour. You can return to your last known place. In the event of cold weather, you have the option of lighting a fire, but did you bring fire-starting materials? Forested areas bring a greater possibility of problem animals, such as snakes (don't collect firewood at night and do be aware of rattling noises) or bears (be noisy on the trail and in camp, camp away from food hangs, hang food high or use bear-proof containers that are away from kitchen areas, carry bear spray, and practice as a group for bear encounters). Other animal problems can be critters eating anything with salt on it, such as boots, helmet straps, wet suits, and climbing ropes, so always zip everything up inside tents. Do not hang them on branches.

Skills and Equipment Needed

Outdoor living skills include hiking, tent selection, campsite selection, food protection skills, food preparation skills, navigation skills, and wilderness first-aid skills. Equipment includes backpacks, stoves, cook pots, water filters, cook tarps, sleeping pads, sleeping bags, flashlights, camp chairs, trowels, and first-aid kits. Boots can be lighter weight, but breathable boots won't stay that way for long, as they get dirty quickly. Also, breathable boots don't stay waterproof for long on snow.

DESERTS
Must-Knows

Many desert plants can impale you, and some also have poisonous saps.

Deserts may be easier to navigate, but your navigation must be accurate to make sure you find that spring when you need water. Also, you might need to negotiate ravines, canyons, and gullies. Those plants you need to wade through—will you be picking spines out of your skin because you didn't wear long pants or sturdy boots? Many desert plants can impale you, and some also have poisonous saps. Will you suffer from sunstroke because you didn't take a wide-brimmed hat and enough water? Planning for water drops as well as food drops will often be necessary. This entails dropping food or water resupplies along your route in secure containers, possibly with the help of an outfitting company. Many problem animals live in deserts, including snakes, spiders, lizards, sand flies, and centipedes. Are you checking your boots for scorpions before you put them on? Campsite selection requires care so that you avoid places that can flash flood. Although rainfall is unusual in deserts, rains there can be torrential. You should *not* be canyoneering if that happens.

An obvious hazard is the heat, so traveling early is a consideration in trip planning. Cold deserts do exist, though, such as in Antarctica, the Arctic, and Greenland.

Skills and Equipment Needed

*Why is that spring
called "Red Ass Spring"?*

Hiking and backpacking skills are required but with some differences to adjust to the desert context. No high trees may be available for hanging food, so you may need plastic containers to keep out critters, such as raccoons and rodents. Clothing may be lighter, but still avoid cotton, as you will sweat, and this is better wicked away by a man-made fiber. Evenings can still be very cold, so plan for a range of temperatures. Planning for water is important—are there springs? Why is that spring called "Red Ass Spring"? So do you have good filtration systems and chemical treatments? Have you organized water drops for areas where no springs can be found? Do you have a wide-brimmed hat, long sleeves, and long pants for protection from the sun and plants? Are your boots substantial enough to protect you from spiky plants? Navigation skills are important because wandering around lost with a finite water supply would be a disaster.

CAVES
Must-Knows

If light sources die, then visibility would be zero, making an exit from a cave without a constructed path nearly impossible.

While caves have some hazards that are similar to mountain activities, such as climbing and scrambling, they also offer some distinct hazards. Of course, visibility is critical, so taking light sources is a necessity. If light sources die, then visibility would be zero, making an exit from a cave without a constructed path nearly impossible. Good navigation in a cave is critical, as time is limited, depending on the life of the batteries keeping your light sources going. Modern lights last much longer than they did in the past, but backup light sources are still always necessary.

CAVING
AN UNDERGROUND MOVEMENT

Caves can be in different types of rock, such as sandstone and limestone, but they are more commonly found in limestone. Limestone caves have vertical fissures (rifts) and horizontal fissures (bedding planes), tubes, small and large stream passages (some wet and some dry), drops, potholes, boulder chokes (where boulders are jammed together), lakes, ducks, sumps (where one needs to duck or dive underwater), and waterfalls. Skills needed include walking, climbing, crawling, squeezing through tight spaces, bridging (across rifts), swimming, wire ladder techniques, rappelling, and rope ascending. Temperatures in caves are usually constant—generally about 50°F (10°C) in northern climates at low altitude but cold enough for hypothermia to develop if the caver stops moving. Wet caves that require rappelling down waterfalls and swimming in cold water require the use of wetsuits. Caves can flood during times of high rainfall, so an eye to the weather is always necessary.

Skills and Equipment Needed

Protective oversuits and knee and elbow pads are needed in sporting caves to protect from abrasions and mud. As many caves are muddy and slippery, good rubber boots with effective treads are necessary. Caves don't harbor a lot of wildlife, but bats are the main hazard, as they can carry rabies and other viruses. Vertical caving requires total reliance on equipment for rappels and ascents, so good equipment and the skilled use of it in descending and ascending are essential.

It is more uncommon to camp in caves, but longer expeditions do camp, and some cavers occasionally do overnights. One difference with this type of camping is that all waste—even human waste—must be removed from the cave in plastic containers or WAG (Waste Alleviation Gelling) Bags. These are also used in fragile environments, such as desert areas, highly frequented mountain areas, and river corridors. Select your clothing and sleeping bags while keeping in mind that caves are usually wet environments. Specialized equipment includes electron ladders, ropes, carabiners, ascenders, descenders, harnesses, helmets, oversuits, wet suits, knee pads, gloves, and boots. Of course, spare lights, batteries, and a first-aid kit are also necessary. Beginners should go with a guide, as getting lost in a cave as a beginner can be a terrifying experience. For the more experienced, a detailed cave survey and compass are necessary. It is common for cavers to learn caves by accompanying more seasoned cavers.

RIVERS
Must-Knows

Most drownings are the result of not wearing a life jacket.

Rivers offer significant hazards, as mishaps can cause a person to be underwater, which, for most people, leaves less than two minutes to rectify the situation. Three extremely important considerations are the ability to swim, a correctly cinched life jacket, and the knowledge and ability to keep one's feet up when swimming. Most drownings are the result of not wearing a life jacket. Many others are the result of someone putting their feet down when in fast water and getting a foot entrapped, the person being pushed down by the force of the current. The force is considerable, and the only way out is for someone else to pull that person back upstream (often an impossible task in under two minutes). A life jacket will not bring you to the surface in this situation. Other hazards include obstructions in the river, such as boulders, undercut ledges, sieves, and trees. The river itself forms hazards from its falling over drops, hydraulics such as holes or stoppers (where the current flows back on itself, creating a "hole" with no exit except perhaps down to the riverbed), whirl-pools, and waves. Rivers vary in difficulty and are graded by the severity of the hazards (classes/grades I through V). Sometimes the rapids are long and continuous, causing "flush" drownings. This is where the boater capsizes and takes a long swim, often in turbulent white water, where they have to time taking their breaths when they pop to the surface after being submerged by waves and hydraulics. This becomes more difficult the longer they need to do this, as they lose strength. It is also compounded by cold water, which saps strength as well. Beginners should start on lakes and grades I and II rivers and progress to higher levels of difficulty only with corresponding increases in skill levels.

It doesn't take much of a drop for a low-head dam to become a "drowning machine" where the current recirculates back upstream.

Rivers change drastically when in flood, often increasing their difficulty level but also potentially taking the unwary paddler into the trees. Add to that floating trees, branches, and other flotsam that paddlers will need to avoid. The river will now also become brown as the flooding churns up sediment in the river, thus reducing visibility in the water and potentially hiding many hazards. Flood stages also increase the power of hydraulics at the base of dams, sometimes called low-head dams. It doesn't take much of a drop for a low-head dam to become a "drowning machine" where the current recirculates back upstream. All low-head dams need to be assessed as to whether the hydraulics below them create such a drowning machine, as many do.

Skills and Equipment Needed

Boating down rivers can be done in kayaks, canoes, rafts, duckies (inflatable kayaks), or tubes or on stand-up paddleboards. The equipment has become very specialized, so the boater can play in the various river features, run different kinds of rivers, or paddle lakes or the ocean. An additional useful safety skill is for the paddler to be able to roll the kayak or canoe from being upside down after a capsize (also called an Eskimo roll or kayak roll) rather than having to "wet exit" (to pull off the spray skirt covering the top of the boat to prevent water from coming in and to allow exit from the boat into the water) and then swim.

> *Being able to do a "wet exit" from a kayak, which entails pulling off the spray skirt and leaning forward to exit the boat, is an essential skill.*

The skill level of the paddler is critical for safety, as higher skill levels can prevent the need to swim and self-rescue (getting the boat and paddle to the shore in the event of a swim). Being able to do a kayak roll is by far safer than exiting the boat and swimming. It is accomplished by pushing the paddle to the surface when upside down and sweeping it out to the side

while at the same time rotating the boat by kicking up hard with the knee and hips (sometimes called a hip flick). A modified version can also be done in a canoe. The skill requires coordination and technique rather than strength and is best learned in a class in a swimming pool.

Swift water rescue skills are also required to provide help for fellow paddlers. A rescue kit of ropes, webbing, and carabiners is essential, but you also need the skill to use them. Paddlers often paddle year-round now with the availability of wet suits and dry suits. These items are essential to wear in the winter, as cold water can immobilize anyone immersed in it for even a short time.

LAKES

Must-Knows

As with rivers, it is essential to wear a properly cinched life jacket when on or in a lake. Often, because it is "only" a lake, paddlers will get lax with this. If you are a nonswimmer or a weak swimmer, then your life is greatly at risk if you flip whatever craft you are in or on. Or what if everyone in your group is a good swimmer but the lake is large and cold? Your choice of taking a route down the middle of the lake may not be a good one if the water temperature is very cold, as someone or everyone may succumb to hypothermia before getting to shore or if you have to do a self-rescue in the event of a capsize.

Another hazard for the lake paddler is wind. Some lakes, such as Lake Shoshone in Yellowstone National Park, have predictable and consistent wind, so everyone moves about on it in the early morning when it is calm. For other lakes, the wind may not be predictable, so there may be no paddling until the wind dies down. Kayaks fare better for paddling in windy conditions than canoes or paddleboards, as they have less "windage," or area for the wind to push.

Skills and Equipment Needed

Critical skills to have include efficient paddle strokes to enable paddling in a straight line and deep-water rescues. If in a kayak, being able to roll is the best self-rescue skill. Some boats are easier to roll than others. Recreational boats have large cockpits and no thigh grips, so they can't be rolled back up. There are several designs of kayaks for lakes—some recreational to enable fishing and others more streamlined, such as sea kayaks, to better cope with the wind. Canoes are larger and can carry more equipment if you are camping. Another hazard to avoid is lightning, so it is critical to keep a watch on the weather.

SEAS

Must-Knows

All lake hazards can also be experienced on the sea. However, the Las Vegas odds of something dire happening on the sea are increased significantly. The wind that felt moderate when you started out could increase and start blowing offshore, so do you have the strength to paddle against it if this happens? If you are in a group, can you stay together to help each other out? Do you have navigational equipment so that when the fog and mist come down, you can still proceed to the correct destination? Do you have a kayak that is designed for the sea? For example, some kayaks have rudders that enable them to track better in varying wind and wave conditions.

Are you practiced in doing a deep-water rescue in difficult sea conditions? A strong Eskimo roll is a real advantage—but can you do it in savage sea conditions? Hazards other than the cold, wind, and storms include large waves, breaking waves, races (tidal

SEA KAYAKING

currents off headlands and between landmasses), and overfalls. Overfalls are rapids at sea; they occur where there is a drop in the seabed that produces a large rapid where there is a strong tidal current. Mix these waves up with wind waves, and conditions can be very alarming. So paddling on the ocean can be easy in calm conditions but can escalate to being too much very quickly. Strength, paddling skills, rolling skills, and rescue skills are particularly important.

Another sea activity is surfing. The surf can be small and warm, as in coastal South Carolina, or it can be large and cold, as in the North Sea. Australia has a huge surf as well as dangerous critters, such as the poisonous blue-ringed octopus, jellyfish, sharks, and stingrays. The most common hazard for surfers is rip currents. A rip current occurs when all the water that has reached a beach heads back out to sea. Swimmers know that they are in a rip current when they are swimming to shore but realize they are making no progress. If you are caught in a rip current, stop heading directly toward the beach and head sideways for a while, then head toward the beach once you are out of the rip current.

Sometimes on steeply shelving beaches, the water can run back very powerfully after hitting the sand. This undertow can pull you off your feet and into deep water. This is dangerous especially for small children who might simply be walking around at the edge of the surf. Another hazard can be the type of wave. Nice surfing waves roll in, but some waves build up and drop. These are called "dumpers," as they drop a considerable weight of water directly on top of the surfer. These are more dangerous, and it is not advisable to ride them. Surfboarders do not tend to wear life jackets, while kayakers (and canoeists) do for the most part. Collisions with kayakers are also possible, as surfers may travel at 40 miles per hour down a wave. Surfboarders tend to go along the wave, whereas boaters who are not in surf kayaks go more directly down the wave. This scenario creates more chances for collisions. A good policy to avoid collisions is judicious timing in going for a wave and for the kayaker to do an Eskimo roll if a collision looks likely. The body's dragging underwater during the roll stops or slows the kayak considerably. Hitting someone with a pointy kayak can result in internal injuries. Wherever possible, boarders and boaters should try to surf away from each other.

Skills and Equipment Needed

Strong paddle strokes are necessary for making headway against any type of wind. A group should always have the skills to conduct a deep-water rescue in case of a capsize. Eskimo rolls are useful for advanced sea kayaking where rescues are difficult. Being able to do a wet exit from a kayak is an essential skill. Leaning back often inhibits the exit, and a life jacket often pushes one back, so practice doing a wet exit initially with someone standing close by to assist if necessary. Rolling is an essential skill for kayak or canoe surfing, as surfing often results in frequent flips. You don't want to spend the day continually emptying out your boat on the beach. Specialized surf kayaks are available, but many people still use river kayaks and canoes. For the open ocean, something much longer is needed, and specialized sea kayaks are available that are long and that track well, often with rudders. The type of clothing needed, as is the case on lakes and rivers, will depend on air and water temperature because, in the event of a capsize, hypothermia can set in within minutes when it is cold. Paddlers often wear wet suits and dry suits to protect against the cold, and when surfing, canoeists and kayakers wear helmets as well. The use of life jackets is standard practice, and first-aid supplies should be carried. Other safety equipment needed includes a rope for towing, whistles, and emergency beacons.

PREVENTION TECHNIQUES

If that onshore wind changes to an offshore one when you are on the ocean, do you have the strength to paddle back to land?

The goal is to prevent getting into a survival situation, so it is important to look at the potential hazards of each environment separately while keeping in mind that conditions in all environments are fluid. The environment changes with temperature, weather, and group dynamics. In the afternoon, rockfall in the mountains is more likely as the sun melts the ice holding the rock together, and travel is more difficult if you are sinking deeper into the snow. Heavy rain can change rivers dramatically, or it can turn some caves into death traps as they flood to the roof. If that onshore wind changes to an offshore one when you are on the ocean, do you have the strength to paddle back to land?

Do you have the correct clothing and equipment for the area you are visiting? For example, if you are from the southern United States and intend to winter camp in Minnesota, then you need to do serious research on what to bring along. Should you first go with someone who has had that experience or go with an outfitter/guide from the local area? The answer is probably yes.

You may come from Minnesota and have both cold- and hot-weather skills (Minnesota summers are very hot), but what environmental differences are there if you head south for backpacking or canoeing in Texas? You need to be sure that you can get water and that you have sturdy boots and long pants for protection against seriously spiky plants.

Are encounters with animals likely in the place you intend to go?

Are encounters with animals likely in the place you intend to go (e.g., bears, mountain lions, scorpions, snakes, porcupines, skunks, raccoons, moose, or wild bulls)? Have you practiced drills for possible confrontations, and can you protect your food and gear?

Remember that, besides food, animals also like the salt on your boots, wet suits, and ropes, and some critters just like to steal things. I had a band of raccoons come into a "Megamid"-type shelter (a type of tent where the shelter doesn't connect to the floor tarp) and steal a backpack and assorted climbing gear. Fortunately, I woke up and chased them up a trail before they got too far, and, luckily, they dropped everything. I have experienced a porcupine settle down inside my tent, so make sure you zip those doors closed unless you want a spiky snuggle. I have heard skunks rolling around students' bodies lying under a tarp because they didn't hang their GORP ("good old-fashioned raisins and peanuts" or trail mix). Those students had to act as though they were "statues" until the skunks decided to move on to prevent an unpleasant spraying incident. I have even been chased by an emu in Georgia after it had escaped from an emu farm. And we have had boots, helmet chin straps, and ropes chewed through when they were left out at night. If you are in the United States and you hear a rattle, assume it is a rattlesnake and not a cicada. Sea kayakers have had seabirds throw up on them for encroaching on their domain. Of course, the most feared critters are bears, with good reason, so be religious about following bear protocols—be noisy on the trail and in camp, have clean kitchens but store food in bear containers or hang food, cook far away from tents, and carry bear spray.

Do you have the technical skills for the activity you are doing and the skills for a possible evacuation?

Are you taking satellite phones or safety beacons with you? Do you have the knowledge for dealing with specialized injuries for that particular environment? Luckily, if the answer is no, there are courses you can take for all these different activities.

Remember:
1. Use good judgment.
2. Be here now.
3. Everything takes a lot longer than you think.
4. Look at the Las Vegas odds of bad consequences.
5. Know what you know and know what you don't know.

Climate, Weather, Clothing, and Energy

Will where you're going be cold, warm, or hot? What are the expected problems related to the climate you are visiting, such as storms, rain, snow, and so on? Which clothing is suitable for the activity and the climate? What will your energy needs be to combat heat and cold injuries—are you taking enough food and water?

We can't control the climate and weather when venturing outside, but we can control its effects. Traveling to an unfamiliar climate could mean you're in for a big surprise. The temperature can be many degrees below freezing—add in wind chill, and you are in Arctic conditions. When going to an unfamiliar climate, it is a good idea to research what it will be like so that you know what to expect and can prepare for the potential weather you might encounter. The weather accounts for many injuries and deaths in the wild outdoors. An example from Grand Teton National Park in Wyoming is as follows: "Rescue on the Grand Teton in 2010. Seventeen climbers in three separate climbing groups required assistance because of a thunderstorm with lightning strikes."[1]

Kelsey Dayton, a staff writer at the *Star-Tribune*, wrote in the previously mentioned article about the incident: "They didn't know that the weather had already made a plan of its own," referring to the fact that the climbers had started early with the intention of being back in camp by noon to avoid afternoon storms. However, moisture coming from the south fueled the thunderstorms. "Injuries from the thunderstorm included several people that were paralyzed, someone was blasted off the mountain, several people's flesh was burned—including from a watch burned into someone's flesh—and someone's ring finger exploded. It called for the largest rescue in the park's history."

You don't have to be on a mountaintop to be in danger from a lightning strike. In a 1951 incident in nearby Darby Canyon, also in the Tetons, five people from the Darby Girls' Camp were killed and nine injured. "They picked the perfect spot for our lunch," wrote one survivor. At least it was what they perceived to be the perfect spot. The survivor continued, "It was under a Balsam Pine." However, lightning hit the tree they sat under.[2]

A hiking incident in the Lake District in England was less dramatic but could have ended up being equally deadly. A local news article reported that a hiker was suffering from hypothermia on Scafell Pike when she was advised to descend to keep warm and escape heavy winds:

> Once her condition had been established, it was pointed out that staying put at high level in strong

> wind was likely making things worse, and the [res-
> cue] team were likely to be nearly an hour getting to
> them. She warmed some by descending and getting
> to lower ground and warmer temperatures.[3]

Meanwhile, in 1963 on Lake Hume in Australia, two instructors for the organization Outward Bound and five students died because of a squall overturning canoes. "The two instructors helped four youths ashore then returned to aid others. However, their own craft overturned throwing them into the near freezing water."[4]

Outside Online reported the second most deadly North American mountaineering accident, which occurred in 1986 on Mount Hood when seven students and two teachers from a school group died during a huge storm on the mountain. "Weather services had predicted a multi-day storm with 'vicious winds' and heavy moisture coming in from the sea."[5]

MUST-KNOWS

Looking at the accidents discussed in this chapter, it is clear that weather is a critical component in creating survival situations, so the decision has to be made about whether to go or stay and, if the decision is made to go, what preparation will be needed. Failure to assess the forecast and heed its warnings can, has, and will force many people into survival situations. So let us look at the following variables to consider: elements of weather, environmental injuries, and weather forecasting (i.e., the results of injuries caused by weather).

ELEMENTS OF WEATHER

Temperature

• The highest temperature of the day is usually reached by 2 p.m., so determine which activity you anticipate doing at that time and decide whether it is a good plan for the day's high temperature. Wading through snow, for example, could potentially be a bad plan, as it could be soft in spring mountaineering situations. Summer hiking at this time could also be too hot. This is sometimes a good time for a nap if you have had an "alpine start" at 4 a.m. or earlier.

We should have left at 4 am!

DEEP SNOW HIKE

• The lowest night temperature occurs just before sunrise. This can provide easier walking on snow if the snow is still hard.

• For every 1,000 feet in elevation gain, the temperature drops 3°F. As you climb a mountain, it will become colder, so don't anticipate that the temperature at the top will be the same as it is at the trailhead. Wind chill makes it feel even colder.

• Freezing temperatures can produce verglas. Verglas is a thin coating of ice on an exposed surface. It is often clear and can be covered with snow. Stepping onto verglas without crampons could result in a fall. And did you remember to bring your ice axe?

Humidity

• Humidity refers to evaporated water in gaseous form in the air.

• The amount of vapor plus the temperature determines the degree of humidity.

• When the moisture reaches saturation, condensation or precipitation occurs. Light condensation is mist, and denser condensation is fog (clouds are usually fog at higher altitude). In addition to the cooling effects on your body temperature from becoming wet, your visibility will be affected as well, meaning that you'll need to use a compass. Frequent trips over the moors in Yorkshire, where visibility was sometimes only about 20 feet, gave us good practice at navigating in thick fog by compass and not by sight as we tried to aim for two rock monoliths called "Jenny Twig" and her daughter "Tibb" (supposedly two witches who had been "changed to stone") while also avoiding deep bogs flagged by sphagnum moss. If you can't see your target, then send someone ahead until you can just be seen by them so that you can adjust their position to be on the bearing. Repeat this until you reach your planned target. Avoid the bogs by using "doglegs" around them (head 90° out for enough paces, resume the bearing, head 90° back, and resume the bearing).

• Precipitation could be rain, snow, hail, or sleet, depending on air temperature.

• When warm air contacts cold objects, it causes condensation. Examples include warm breath on a sleeping bag; dew on the grass, a tent, or a sleeping bag (if outside); or, if below freezing, frost. If you are considering sleeping under the stars, what are the chances of a heavy dew? This could mean a wet sleeping bag. If you seal the vents in your tent, you may get wet through condensation. If five people are in your tent, the amount of condensation will increase significantly, so make sure the vents are open.

Winds

• In clear weather, air will rise during the day, causing a valley breeze.

• On clear nights, mountains without a cloud cover cool down, and the heavier, colder air slides down the valleys. This can affect where you decide to camp. In one site in the Tetons, we chose the downhill side of some trees that acted as a windbreak because the wind could be both cold and ferocious. In the Blue Ridge Mountains in February, we avoided what was a beautiful campsite because it was in a deep hollow next to the river and therefore extremely cold.

• Wind can affect activities such as canoeing or kayaking. Shoshone Lake in Yellowstone National Park has very powerful winds, but the air is still early in the mornings, so that is when canoeists switch campsites. Wind can be powerful enough to prevent progress in a canoe and can capsize them, especially during squalls.

• Wind can be powerful enough to blow individuals off cliffs. On some occasions in the Lake District in England, we had to rope students together to protect against this.

• Wind increases the possibility of hypothermia. This is especially a risk if you are wet because the ensuing evaporation cools the body down even more.

Mountain Weather

• Mountain weather can be local, such as summer storms that come on most afternoons. An example is Mount Cook in New Zealand.

Snow

• In the western United States at 5,000 feet or higher, it is possible that snow can fall at any time of the year. Excessive snowfall brings avalanches, for which your survival time is only around 20 minutes if you become buried. You most often cannot self-extricate, as the snow sets up solid when it stops.

• Warm weather in snow country can create problems, such as melting snow bridges, rising streams, and avalanches caused by cornices breaking off or by heavy, wet snow on top of prior unstable surfaces. Cornices are snow overhangs caused by snow blowing over ridges. Streams that were passable before any thaw become impassable with all the extra water from the snowmelt.

Lightning

• Lightning is the visible result of an electrical discharge within a cloud or between a cloud and the earth.

• A lightning bolt may release up to 300 million volts.

• Thunder is the atmospheric compression wave that accompanies the electrical discharge.

Phenomena Preceding a Strike

• Thunderheads (large, black cumulonimbus clouds). If these start to build, you should head down the mountain if you are at a higher elevation. You should be back in camp by noon or 2 p.m. at the latest—before they build. This means you will need to do "alpine starts" (4 a.m. rise or earlier).

• St. Elmo's fire is a visible corona or discharge around pointed objects, such as trees or summit blocks (a bluish glow). If it is on your ice axe or helmet, then it is time to say your prayers!

• Your hair is standing on end.

LIGHTNING

Precautions

• Don't be the highest thing in the area. Examples are a hiker in an open meadow, a climber on a summit or ridge, a boater on a lake, or anyone out in the open or under a lone tree or a high tree.

• In the woods, choose to be around smaller trees.

• Have the group spread out so that there are some survivors to assist any casualties.

• Don't be under rock overhangs so that you become a "spark plug." A deep cave is fine as long as you are not in any water.

• Don't lie down because of ground currents. Crouch or sit on something that is insulated.

• Being in an automobile is good because of the rubber tires and the "Faraday cage" effect, which spreads the current out around you. The electrical field inside the cage is canceled as the electrical charge is conducted around it.

• Don't stand next to metal fences. People have been killed by currents coming from miles away.

• Don't use plug-in telephones (not likely these days but still a possibility).

Prevention Techniques
Aside from the specifics for lightning detailed earlier, you should research the area you intend to visit and take appropriate gear and clothing. Minnesota winter camping requires different items than winter

camping in North Carolina, where, for example, felt boots aren't necessary. A cagoule (a lightweight, hooded, thigh-length waterproof jacket) could be handy in North Carolina, where it may rain constantly for days at a time, whereas something breathable would be better in the Minnesota winter, where it would most likely be snow and not constant rain.

Researching problems specific to the area is a good thing, especially by asking people who have done similar activities there. However, some things do change over time. We always recommended down (or imitation down) booties to students going on outdoor courses in June in the Tetons because we usually spent considerable amounts of time standing or sitting in snow kitchens while preparing dinners, lunches, and breakfasts. The down booties were great to get into after spending the day in big boots. More recently, overboots were necessary as well, as it is not as cold in June as it used to be; so, because the snow is more slushy and wet, down boots do not work well. Attending a course in the area you would like to operate is a great way to learn, or you can take a guide who has been there before. For traveling on snow, knee-high gaiters for attaching to your boots are necessary. They are usually attached with a strap under the boot. Have you made sure that the buckles are on the outside of the feet as opposed to being on the inside, where they can catch and cause you to trip? Gaiters also work well in conjunction with cagoule-style raincoats, as they prevent water dripping into boots. They also prevent twigs and debris from getting into your boots in the woods or your bootlaces coming undone while bush pushing.

Knowing the interactions between the climate, the weather, clothing, food, and water can prevent what are known as environmental injuries, such as hypothermia, frostbite, hyperthermia, and trench foot.

ENVIRONMENTAL INJURIES

Understanding environmental injuries is key to avoiding survival situations. You can prevent hypothermia by knowing that inappropriate clothing such as jeans and other cotton garments, has poor insulating qualities, especially when wet, and thus can result in drops in body temperature. Alternatively, not wearing a hat, not drinking lots of water, and traveling during the hotter parts of the day can result in heat exhaustion and heatstroke. Eating and drinking also provide the fuel you need to help prevent cold exposure. So knowing the interactions between the climate, the weather, clothing, food, and water can prevent what are known as environmental injuries, such as hypothermia, frostbite, hyperthermia, and trench foot. Knowing the weather forecast is also paramount to help you make the right decision on whether to go or stay based on the weather.

WEATHER FORECASTING

The time to be concerned about the weather is not at the first rumble of thunder or the first snowfall but *before* you leave home. Examples of people venturing out into storms and disasters ensuing are many. If you are on a 30-day trip in the Tetons in June, then you may still be out in the elements but could "hole up" in camp (with four-season tents) until the storm passes by, as we have done many times. Hot chocolate is a good trick to help with group dynamics for those three-day storms. But you wouldn't still persevere with the summit day that you may have originally planned. You would stay in camp and prepare awesome meals, drink hot chocolate, build snow caves for fun, and do activities to keep the group motivated.

Careful study of the weather should be done before you go, but it can also be done when you are already in the outdoors either directly through smart phones or by calling someone at home who has access.

If you cannot reach anyone for information about the weather because of damaged equipment or a lack of batteries, then you can use indicators such as clouds. However, as Paul Petzoldt used to say, "Only fools and dudes predict the weather."[6] By this, he meant that as weather is often unpredictable, you better be prepared with the correct clothing and equipment.

The time to be concerned about the weather is not at the first rumble of thunder or the first snowfall but before you leave home.

Weather Indicators

"Red sky at night, sailors' delight; red sky in the morning, sailor's warning," or so goes the old saying. Low humidity results in the most vibrant sky colors; conversely, high humidity mutes sky colors.

Coronas are small rings around the sun or moon. If they are larger, they are called halos. They are caused by moisture coming or departing.

When those fair-weather, harmless-looking white fluffy cumulus clouds start to build, go vertical, and turn black, a thunderstorm is probably heading your way.

For simplicity's sake, *clouds* can be divided into different layers: high, middle, and low. High clouds, such as the wispy cirrus clouds, often indicate bad weather coming or going. Middle clouds (altostratus and altocumulus) indicate the possibility of rain in 8 to 10 hours. Low clouds (fog, stratus, and stratocumulus) don't necessarily produce rain, but when they are black (nimbostratus), it is usually raining. Cumulonimbus clouds, or thunderheads, are the critical clouds to be able to recognize, as they are the ones that indicate you should probably return to camp as they start to build. When those fair-weather, harmless-looking white fluffy cumulus clouds start to build, go vertical, and turn black, a thunderstorm is probably heading your way.

Prevention Techniques

As weather, whether hot or cold, can cause potentially deadly environmental injuries, such as heatstroke and hypothermia, you must consider weather conditions before heading into the wild outdoors. Besides avoiding environmental injuries, it can make travel more efficient by choosing to go at the best time of day for the location, such as going in the early morning when the temperature is lowest when traveling on snow. Researching the area where you intend to travel for the expected temperatures and local weather will enable you to take appropriate gear and clothing. Not taking a four-season tent to the Tetons in early June, for example, could result in a flattened tent under wet, heavy snow. Not taking a wide-brimmed hat and lots of water could result in heatstroke in a desert environment. Walking out into a storm has led to many deaths. Study the weather forecast and decide accordingly to either not go, turn back, or, if a storm is forecasted, stay in the camp.

Ask people who have been to the environment where you are going and *listen carefully* to their advice. Develop a good climate control plan, such as taking good gear and clothing for the place you are going, to enable your personal climate to stay at comfortable levels.

ENERGY

Having enough food and water in your pack is one thing, but are you stopping regularly to actually eat and drink?

So what does energy have to do with weather? Both the energy to keep you warm and the energy to move come from the same "tank"—your own physiology and what you have consumed in water and food—so advance planning is necessary. Are you taking enough food and water with you, and do you have enough nutrients? Many people venture out without sufficient water or without ways to treat the water that may be available.

Having enough food and water in your pack is one thing, but are you stopping regularly to actually eat and drink? Many groups head out on the trail without a plan for regular stops and then find that some of their members "flake out" because they lost energy or got hypothermia or heatstroke. In groups, it can be useful to have such travel roles as the following:

• *Leader*, who monitors the whole group and makes decisions based on the group's needs

• *Scout*, who navigates (and should be checked by everyone else in the group)

• *Pace setter* and *smoother*, who sets a reasonable pace on the trail and makes shortcuts in off-trail situations so that the whole group doesn't, for example, need to follow the scout through a bog

• *Logger*, who notes time spent on travel and rest stops and tips off the leader when it is time to stop or go

• *Sweep*, who checks that no one falls behind the group (and then becomes lost on their own)

This list may seem overly organized, but it enables groups to travel very efficiently. One of the jobs of the leader and logger is to check that you stop at predetermined time intervals, such as half an hour, 45 minutes, or an hour, to *eat and drink* in addition to resting. The logger tips the leader off when it is time to leave (after, say, 10 minutes). The sweep also checks the area for anything left, such as penknives, water bottles, and trash. Rest stops are critical for everyone to refuel and adjust clothing for their personal climate control. It is also psychologically easier for everyone to know that there will be regular rest stops.

Going slow and acclimatizing is preferable to rushing but then needing to stop for a long period to recover. On steep ground, rhythmic breathing and the rest step can be used to help preserve energy. With rhythmic breathing, you consciously take breaths, say, one per step, or, as may be necessary at higher altitudes, two or three per step to get more oxygen to the muscles. With the rest step, used on steep ground, you step up and lock one leg straight so that you use your leg bones rather than your leg muscles to hold your weight.

Paul Petzoldt was a proponent of all these energy-saving techniques and for advance planning. He suggested calculating "energy miles" as a way to not only count the distance to travel but also incorporate the elevation to climb.[7] His formula was to add two miles for every 1,000 feet to be climbed, so if you are planning a hike of three miles with 1,000 feet of elevation, it would be counted as five energy miles. In other words, the hike would be the equivalent energy of doing five miles on the flat. Thinking in energy miles means that you are less likely to over-reach on your planning and not be able to reach your destination.

Remember:
1. Use good judgment.
2. Be here now.
3. Everything takes a lot longer than you think.
4. Look at the Las Vegas odds of bad consequences.
5. Know what you know and know what you don't know.

Problem Wildlife

How do you avoid problems with the local flora and fauna?

If you are going into the wild outdoors, you are going to meet up with wild animals and bump into problem plants. I have experienced proximity to a blue-ringed octopus, a stingray, a jellyfish, barracuda, bears, moose, porcupines, raccoons, snakes, skunks, alligators, mosquitoes, blackflies, midges, and a frisky emu. Some encounters were humorous when in hindsight, such as the escaped emu running at us in the Georgia woods (we fended him off with a stick), the raccoons that came into my shelter and tried to steal my backpack and climbing gear (I caught them dragging my gear up the trail in the middle of the night), and the skunks rolling over my students under a tarp because they had left their GORP out. I did get stung once by stepping on a stingray and was luckily warned by the lifeguards about the blue-ringed octopus one of the kids in our canoe club had placed in a jar. There were loads of them looking like small pieces of granite on the beach in Victoria, Australia. Some incidents were potentially dangerous, as we did trips in the Tetons in June just after the bears were finishing hibernation, so we were especially careful about being noisy on the trail or bush pushing through willow so as not to surprise any bears or moose. We hung food high and downhill of our campsites, and our kitchens were away from our tents. When I lived in Australia, we came across many types of poisonous snakes (and now, living in North Carolina, we have an abundance of copperheads and rattlesnakes). We managed to stay away from them, but we did bump into spiders now and again. We were very careful when mowing the lawn around the 20- by 10-foot web and when pulling the kayaks out from the back shed. We always sprayed the insides of the kayaks with insecticide to lure the spiders out while we drove to the river.

On occasions, critters have been problematic because they like salt and ate through ropes, the tops of boots, and climbing helmet straps, so we learned to keep all that inside zipped tents. We had a porcupine

PORCUPINES

chew up our wet suits one time for the same reason and once had a porcupine slip into our small dome tent for a nap.

Fortunately, we saw it, but many spines were left in there as we tried to encourage it out with a large stick, teaching us to always zip up our tent when we left it. Squirrels are master gymnasts and can walk food bag lines, so is your food bag made of substantial enough material to keep them out? Of course, leaving food bags outside on the ground is an open invitation for critters to come for it, and the word gets out quickly, so campsites can become full of night invaders, such as skunks and raccoons.

Problem plants come in all shapes and sizes, but my experience has been mostly with poisonous plants, such as nettles, poison oak, and poison ivy. Stinging nettles are more of a temporary annoyance, although they do cause immediate pain, whereas both poison oak and poison ivy can give longer-term pain with blisters, so wearing protective clothing to avoid contact is key. Not breathing the smoke from their leaves and vines is also important. This means that you need to be able to recognize them. Other plants to avoid are desert plants that often have needle-like spines, meaning you should wear protective clothing and boots. As many plants are poisonous to eat, the recommendation is to not experiment and eat only known, safe varieties after having good training. So for the average person, good planning regarding packing enough food and protecting it from spoilage and theft is paramount.

It is impossible to detail every problem animal or bug (yes, bugs are included) here, but information on many common ones follow.

MUST-KNOWS

The must-knows for problem animals and plants would be to research what potentially dangerous or problematic animals and plants to expect where you intend to go and what the protocols are for dealing with them.

Insects

Wherever you go, there will be bugs—from the Highlands of Scotland to the jungles of South America to the Outback of Australia. Bug-proof netting on your tent is essential, and depending on where you go, a head net or bodysuit may also be necessary. The Scottish Highlands may not have mosquitoes, but they do have midges, or small blackflies that seem to have voracious appetites. Many regions have mosquitoes that sometimes are just bothersome, but others can carry serious diseases, such as West Nile virus, encephalitis, and malaria. Other illnesses, such as Rocky Mountain spotted fever, Colorado tick fever, and Lyme disease, are carried by ticks. When I lived in Australia, an outbreak of Murray Valley encephalitis occurred, and we weren't supposed to go near the river where more mosquitoes were present. We did anyway but covered up more and used insect repellent. Added protection besides clothing could be "bug juice," or insect repellent; the most effective types will contain DEET. In the northeastern United States, we used special tents called "bug-outs" for use in blackfly season, when there are both mosquitos and blackflies to contend with. The bug-out tent had a waterproof roof and fly-proof walls, so you erected it and then killed all the bugs inside. Tick checks should be done regularly so they can be removed as soon as possible.

"Bugs" also occur in many water sources. These are microscopic and include viruses, bacteria, and protozoa, so just taking a drink from a lake or stream could result in gastrointestinal illnesses. We even sterilize our eating and cooking utensils by dipping them in boiling water before use—even though we also wash them with soap and rinse after use. Bugs can also be passed around a group by lack of cleanliness. How many people in the group are not washing their hands after "bathroom" visits and before cooking? Are they sharing mugs and water bottles? This is a great way to pass on germs. A puddle of red water from melting snow could be a result of an algae called *Chlamydomonas nivalis*, which causes the snow to turn pink with a faint smell of watermelon. Eating "watermelon snow" could have a laxative effect, so eating or drinking affected snow or water is not recommended. The woods and the wild outdoors are not the places to be with diarrhea or giardia.

Prevention Techniques

Wear clothing or head nets, bodysuits, and so on to cover skin where possible or use insect repellent where not. Take shelters that have netting to keep bugs out and do tick checks regularly. Treat all water chemically or with a good filter but bear in mind that filters break, so take backup chemical pills. Be as clean as possible with personal hygiene and by washing and sterilizing cooking and eating implements.

Stinging Insects

Stinging insects, such as bees, wasps, and fire ants, can produce allergic or anaphylactic shock reactions. Always take antihistamines, such as Benadryl and epinephrine, in your first-aid kit, and if you know you are allergic, then an EpiPen or two is also advised. Currently, EpiPens are extraordinarily expensive in the United States, so learning how to inject epinephrine without an autoinjector is a possibility, as is seeking generic versions of EpiPens.

Prevention Techniques

Being covered up can help, but often the little stingers are on you when you are hiking in shorts and light clothing. If you are in a group, the last few people in the line are most likely to get stung after the front people have disturbed the nest, which is often underground. Of course, any nests, including those in tree branches, are best left undisturbed. As allergic reactions can be life threatening when airways swell, having epinephrine and some antihistamines to counteract that is critical.

Snakes

> *Know what types of snakes are in the area you are visiting and study what they look like.*

Not all snakes are poisonous, but you could become infected by a bite that is not envenomated, so stay away from all snakes. Some people want to pick them up—which is obviously a bad idea. Listen for rattling if you are in rattlesnake country and assume it is a snake and not an insect if you hear it. Keep your eyes peeled for snakes while walking. They generally attack only when threatened, so you don't want to step on one. They can also be in tree branches. If bitten, the only option you have is to evacuate to a hospital for some antivenin while hoping that you recognized what type of snake it was. Trying to kill it may result in another bite.

Prevention Techniques

Know what types of snakes are in the area you are visiting and study what they look like. For example, in western North Carolina, the two most common venomous snakes are copperheads and rattlesnakes, both of which have diamond-shaped heads, whereas the common black snake doesn't and is not venomous. Wear substantial boots and even possibly gaiters, don't pick up snakes, and don't reach into blind places, such as over logs and into crevices, especially at dusk (e.g., if looking for firewood). I haven't known of snakes slithering under sleeping tarps and shelters, but if you want to be doubly sure, use a sewn-in groundsheet-type tent that is sealed. Keep an eye on the trail and in long grass (i.e., always be in the here and now).

Spiders and Scorpions

All spiders have some venom, but some are especially toxic. Some, such as the black widow, have a nerve toxin that causes muscle spasms, chills, sweating, and severe chest or belly pain. Others, such as the brown recluse, have necrotic venom that destroys cell membranes, resulting in the death of the surrounding tissue.

You might not realize you've been bitten until the spider is long gone. Spiders seem to like dark places and corners to make their webs. Australia has many varieties of spiders that you would not want to bump into. For example, while there, I was advised to lift any toilet seat in outside "dunnies" (toilets) to check for "redbacks" (black widows) or other possible biters. Besides redbacks, trapdoor spiders, huntsman, tarantulas, and funnel web spiders, among others, can be found in Australia. Having seen a picture of a pair of envenomated testicles, I would take the "dunny" advice seriously.

Scorpions make up many species, some more poisonous than others. Recognizing the differences can be difficult, so avoid contact if possible.

Prevention Techniques

Don't poke around in dark places, do the dunny seat check even when you are not in a dunny, wear gloves for gathering firewood, and check anything that you are getting into, such as shoes, boots, kayaks, and sleeping bags. Wear insect repellent and spray the insides of kayaks before loading on the car so that critters exit long before you want to get in them. Keep tents fully zipped up all the time to keep scorpions out. Don't try picking them up, check your shoes before putting them on, and shake out your clothes for spiders and scorpions.

Alligators and Crocodiles

Alligators and crocodiles can move very fast on land and in the water. Just because they are basking in the sun and look sleepy doesn't mean they can't lunge and reach you in a split second. Alligators are found in the United States and China, and crocodiles are found in North America, Asia, Australia, and Africa. Crocodiles are more often found in saltwater environments. They can swim up to 20 miles per hour and can run 11 miles per hour.

Prevention Techniques

Stay at least 40 feet away from gators or crocs on land. Don't let children or pets play near the water's edge. Don't swim in gator or croc country. Don't feed them. Stay alert—be in the here and now.

Cougars

Cougars have become more problematic recently as humans encroach more and more on their territories. In general, they stay hidden, but as they like chasing things, mountain bikers and runners are fair game to them. I have never seen one in the wild but have seen tracks in the snow in the Tetons, so we knew they were around us. They are less likely to attack a group than they are an individual. We advised our group members to be social about toilet breaks and to go with a "guard" who also had bear spray. Running away from a cougar would be ineffective and

would encourage a chase. If attacked, the advice is to fight back as best you can.

Bobcats are seldom seen in the eastern United States and are usually detectable only by prints and scat. They don't usually attack humans.

Prevention Techniques
If you know you are in mountain lion country, try to stay together as a group as much as possible. Small youngsters running around could invite an attack. Take a guard with bear spray on toilet visits. Store food in sealed containers away and downwind from tents.

Bears
There are different kinds of bear that require different attitudes. All bears can kill and maim. The obvious problem bears are polar bears and grizzly bears, especially when hungry. Are you going to an area where they are coming out of hibernation and are in fact very hungry? Brown bears or grizzly bears are famous for looking vicious and scary, and recent movies and news reports do generally get people's attention. However, they usually don't seek humans as a food source, and encounters usually are accidental. To prevent accidental encounters, encourage the group to be noisy on the trail and in camp. Bears usually feed at night, so limit activities at that time, even going to the toilet. For those who can, take a "trucker's friend" (a pee bottle) with you so you can pee inside the tent and not have to take a quick trip into

the woods at night. If you do meet up with a bear, do not run, as they will give chase, and you cannot outrun a bear. Have bear spray handy (not packed away in your pack). Learn how to use it and do not spray yourself by accident. You need to keep calm enough so that when faced with a bear, you don't look it in the eye. Rather, stay still, possibly backing off slowly. If it charges, hit it in the face with the bear spray.

All bears can kill and maim.

The Alaska Department of Fish and Wildlife says that you have two choices if attacked by a bear: play dead or fight back. When a bear is acting defensively, especially brown bears, the department says to play dead:

> Hit the ground and lie still, if a brown bear you have surprised or any female bear protecting cubs makes contact. Lie flat on your stomach, legs spread apart for stability, with your hands protecting the back of your neck. A defensive bear usually ends its attack, if it feels you are not a threat. Remain motionless for as long as possible. If you move, and the bear sees or hears you, it may return and renew its attack. In a prolonged attack, fight back.

But when a bear perceives a human as food, the department says to fight back:

> Rarely, lone black bears or brown bears may perceive a person as potential food. Fight any bear that has been calmly focused on you and makes contact or that breaks into a tent or building. In almost all situations, your best defense against an attacking black bear is to fight back. Concentrate on the bear's face or muzzle with anything you have on hand.[1]

We have chased off lone black bears that were near our campsites, and often they move on. However, if it is a female bear with cubs, this is very dangerous. Give that bear a very wide berth. Climbing trees isn't much help, as black bears can climb very well, grizzlies less so. Bears have a very acute sense of smell and so may find you because of your food.

COME AND GET IT

Cooking bacon or a steak in bear country is like ringing a dinner bell for them, so choose food wisely. Storing food is also important. Use bear-proof containers, electrified fences, or high food hangs (at least 15 feet) that are a good distance from your tents and

kitchens. The food storage should be downhill, as the wind usually blows downhill at night. This will carry any food smells away from the camping area. If you have anything that smells like toothpaste or if you have clothing with spilled food on it, it should be stored with the food and not taken into tents.

Prevention Techniques

Be noisy on the trail to prevent surprise encounters and practice "bear in camp" procedures, where you all get together to look as large as you can and make significant noise. Triangulate your camp, kitchen area, and food storage 100 yards apart if you can. If you are intending to hang food bags, learn how to do it and practice before you go. This is complex—it involves getting ropes over high branches and using trucker's hitches, carabiners, and Z-drags. Will the trees be high enough? At higher altitudes, trees tend to be smaller. Do this as soon as you have erected tents, preferably in the light, as it is hard enough without trying it by flashlight. In other places, there are small trees or no trees, which means you need alternative ways of securing food from not only bears but other animals as well, such as raccoons. Carry bear spray, one canister per person, and know how to use it. If you are practicing and fire off a canister, know that the contents may actually attract bears. To be effective in deterrence, bear spray needs to be fired into the face of the bear. You are more likely to hit a bear with bear spray than with a gun during an attack. Make the decision whether to fight back or play dead. Remember not to run away. Don't roam around at night in the dark. Don't use smelly perfumes or smelly soap and don't keep any food or toothpaste in tents. Choose food that produces the least smell possible.

Wolves, Coyotes, Moose, Bison, and Other Large Animals

Stay away from big wild animals.

Stay away from any big wild animal and, as with bears, be noisy while on the trail and while bush pushing to avoid unexpected encounters. They tend to want to stay away from you, and even though some may look slow, they can easily kill you. Do not get close to take pictures, or you may join the "Last Selfie Club." Getting close to wolves or coyotes is nearly impossible anyway unless they are sick and therefore behaving

friendly or in an unusual manner, which may mean they may have rabies.

Wild Animals Acting Strangely or Friendly

Any wild animal acting friendly should be avoided, as they could be rabid, and a bite could either kill you in an unimaginably horrible way or send you to the hospital for painful vaccinations. This includes raccoons, dogs, cats, bats, and rats.

Hazardous Marine Life: Sharks, Barracuda, Stingrays, Blue-Ringed Octopus, Jellyfish, and More

My experience with marine life is somewhat limited to being mainly a kayaker and snorkeler with only a couple of scuba dives, but I have bumped into all the aforementioned problems. Sharks were always on our minds when I kayaked in the ocean in Australia, so we had "spotters" on the beach looking for fins. In South Carolina, I have seen small sharks being pulled out by fishermen from right where we had been playing around in the surf. Recently, more shark attacks have been reported on the East Coast of the United States, but in general, they are rare. Having stood on a stingray on a nearby beach, I rushed back to the hotel to soak my foot in hot water. The same beaches were cleared at times because of jellyfish. Barracuda merely swam by us, seemingly uninterested, when diving in Mexico and Belize. The blue-ringed octopus that we found on the beach in Australia with its deadly toxin worried us enough that we decided to stick to the rivers and possible nearby snakes and spiders.

Of course, if you venture into places like Greenland, South America, and Africa, there are many killer fish, such as the following:

- The 50-plus-pound pacu from the Amazon with large teeth

- The giant sawfish that lives in rivers and lakes

- The flathead catfish, which weighs in at 120 pounds, from North America

- The payara, which has six-inch fangs, from the Amazon River, along with the better-known piranha

- The Wallago Attu catfish, from Southeast Asia, India, and Afghanistan, which is predatory and has incredible speed (also known as the "lake shark")

- The Atlantic goosefish, weighing more than 70 pounds, with a large, tooth-lined mouth and stomach nearly the size of its body

- The goliath grouper, which grows to 16 feet and up to 1,000 pounds and can swallow a diver

- Giant snakeheads, which are ferocious predators, can be up to four feet long and 50 pounds and can turn on fishermen if caught

- The Greenland shark, which can be 20 feet long and swims in Arctic waters

- The surgeon fish, which swims in tropical waters and has "blades" in its tail capable of slashing arteries[2]

These are only some of the fish and marine animals that are dangerous.

Prevention Techniques

Again, do research on where you are going to check what to expect with regard to wildlife and either stay away from possible predators or have whatever protection you can get for where you are going. Always be "in the moment" in the wild outdoors, as you do share it with wild things.

Plants

As mentioned earlier, some plants can be problematic if touched and some if ingested. Recognizing both types is critical.

Plants Not to Touch

A common plant to encounter is the stinging nettle. The "sting" is caused by the plant injecting you with formic acid but is often relieved by rubbing it with some saliva on an often close-by dock leaf. Nettles are widespread in Europe, Asia, and North America. They can be boiled and used for tea or shampoo.

Urushiol is the oil from poison ivy, poison oak, sumac, and mango trees that affects many people with blisters on their skin. It can be severe. If it gets on your hands, it needs to be washed off before you start touching your face and other regions. Pet cats and dogs sometimes bring it home on their fur, and owners, unaware they have been stroking fur with the oil on it, then touch their faces, and voila, blisters.

Some people are unaffected by the oil. These plants don't grow in Europe but are common in North America, Taiwan, Japan, Korea, and Sakhalin, an island in Russia. Learning what these plants look like can help you avoid them. For example, poison ivy is a vine that can be hanging from trees or growing out of the ground. The leaves can be small or large. It generally doesn't grow above 5,000 feet, but climate change may be affecting that. If any vines are on fire and you breathe in the smoke, it can affect your respiratory system, so don't throw any vines on your campfire.

Some desert plants are protected by pines and razor-sharp thorns. The cholla cactus, for example, can leave broken thorns in you as you brush past it. Each thorn contains porcupine quill–like scales that are very difficult to remove from the skin. Another example is the cat's claw acacia, which can grow as a tree or large shrub. It is sometimes called the "wait a

bit" tree, as you wait to disengage yourself from the cat's claw-like spines. These are but two examples of problem desert plants.

Jungle plants have an array of ways to "nail" passersby. The cannon ball tree from Central and South America has heavy fruits that eventually fall to the ground and, of course, could hit anyone in the way. Even more painful is the Australian suicide plant, the Gympie-Gympie stinking tree of northern New South Wales and Queensland, which is the same family as the common stinging nettle. As with the nettle, it injects its toxin into the skin, but the pain is intense (the worst kind of pain you can imagine) and long lasting. The offending hairs can become airborne and breathed in.

Plants Not to Eat

In times of shortage, it has been common to experiment with wild plants or leaves that are not usually consumed. For example, rhubarb is the famous plant that in World War I was recommended for eating (leaves and all), but the leaves are actually poisonous. The government accidently poisoned people for a time, although, as a lot of leaves are needed to produce harm, the mistake was not discovered for a while. Another example of unintended poisoning was when Chris McCandlass, the subject of Jon Krakauer's book *Into the Wild*, was "living off the land" and ate wild potato seeds that can cause death in "starving young men."[3] He subsequently died. So eating the wrong plant is a serious mistake. Other examples of poisonous plants are the following:

• Castor bean: The source of castor oil but also ricin, a deadly poison. Avoid ingesting any part of the plant.

• Water hemlock, or "poison parsnip": Can cause respiratory failure soon after ingestion.

• Rhododendron and mountain laurel: Both are very toxic.

• Hogweed: Should not even be touched, as the sap can cause burns and blindness if in the eyes and serious illness or death if eaten.

• Holly: Can cause dehydration and diarrhea.

• Pokeweed: Roots, leaves, stems, and berries are poisonous.

Many wild plants are poisonous, so the list goes on—these are just a few examples.

Prevention Techniques

Do your research on where you are going and take protective clothing and treatment gels with you. Be careful about what you put on any fire. Don't eat unknown plants. Get professional education in what wild plants are edible and safe before trying to "live off the land" or supplement food taken out with you. Some poisonous plants look similar to edible plants. Plan all your expeditions well, especially for bringing sufficient food so that you do not run out and need to forage. This includes keeping your food safe from animals by proper hanging and the use of effective plastic containers.

Remember:
1. Use good judgment.
2. Be here now.
3. Everything takes a lot longer than you think.
4. Look at the Las Vegas odds of bad consequences.
5. Know what you know and know what you don't know.

Skills for Hazards and Emergency Procedures

What specific skills are needed to accomplish your goals, such as hiking, camping, cooking, navigating, canoeing, kayaking, climbing, belaying, rappelling, climbing, caving, skiing, snowshoeing, sailing, self-rescuing, rescue techniques, first-response techniques, and so on?

Most activities in the wild outdoors require skills. For example, simply jumping into a kayak and pushing off from the bank could mean that you can't get out when you tip over, perhaps because you did not make sure that the spray skirt release tag was out. Can you swim if you exit the boat? Are you wearing a lifejacket that is well secured?

Do you know how to pack a backpack? Do you know how much water to take with you, how to purify your water, and how far you can hike? Skill development for all activities is critical, so you should not "push off" on your own but rather go with someone who knows what they are doing, hire a qualified guide, or attend a course. You should practice the skills you need in safe environments where failure doesn't mean a serious incident. For example, you should practice on a class II river as a beginner boater after doing pool and lake sessions rather than jumping straight to running class III or higher rivers that have big rapids and serious consequences. Even simple hiking requires some skills. Many people have become lost and run out of water in a valley near where I live in the Blue Ridge Mountains because they took only one bottle of water and had a map but couldn't read it. So let's start with hiking and backpacking.

HIKING

Hiking should be relatively simple, but many incidents arise from basic mistakes, such as not taking any water or enough water and food. They are your energy sources. How much energy is needed for a 10-mile hike? Quite a lot: 10 miles for a beginner is a long way. It is better to start with short hikes of less than five miles. What if elevation gains are significant? That will add both energy and time. Paul Petzoldt suggested adding two miles for every 1,000 feet gained to the miles on the ground and then call them "energy miles" so that you don't miscalculate how far you can travel.[1] Take regular preset breaks so that you and everyone in the group stops to refuel by snacking and drinking water. Using roles when in groups helps this, such as having a leader (who monitors the whole group), a pacesetter/smoother (who keeps the pace slow and cuts unnecessary "corners" if bush pushing), a logger (who notes the time for each leg and rest break), and a sweep (who stays at the back to check that no one falls behind and also checks the rest areas for anything dropped by the group).

In addition to doing good planning that accounts for topographical features, rivers, and other natural hazards, leave a plan of where you are going with someone who is not on the trip and preferably don't go alone. Wear appropriate clothing and footwear. Hiking poles really help. Don't forget a first-aid kit, cell phone, map, and compass and GPS unit or cell phone app while still bearing in mind that all electronics can fail. Boots are critical also; they should be "broken in" before you go on any trip. Any "hot spots" need to be covered with moleskin immediately after they appear. I have seen beginners get blisters within 15 minutes of starting out because they didn't do this. Once a blister forms, it has to be cleaned and dressed frequently and is a considerable hassle (every day), so prevention is very important.

Hiking should be relatively simple, but many incidents arise from basic mistakes, such as not taking any water or enough water and food. They are your energy sources.

CAMPING

Car camping means that you can take a lot of equipment, but you can't get that far away from "civilization." Backpacking means you can get farther into the backcountry, but you need to limit what you take to what you can carry, trying to stay under 30 pounds if you can. Extended expeditions that may require you to also take climbing gear and possibly extra clothing for snow trips means your pack could weigh up to 60 pounds, and such a heavy pack is not for the fainthearted. Usually, you bank on being able to carry only a week's worth of food, and this depends on what kind of food you take. Dehydrated food is lightweight but expensive. Some varieties can be quite tasty. "Total food planning"—taking lots of raw ingredients, such as flour, rice, and pasta, along with a good spice kit—is cheaper and enables creative cooking but is heavier.

Your choice of equipment, such as what type of tent to bring, depends on where you are going. Something light works in many cases but not for, say, springtime in the mountains, when you may get heavy, wet snowfalls that could collapse a three-season tent. If you bought a new tent, are the seams sealed, or do you need to do that? Have you practiced erecting it before you go so that you aren't figuring it out in the middle of a storm? For further comfort, choose a good sleeping pad, perhaps one that is inflatable. You don't have to rough it without a pillow—you can take a pillowcase and stuff it with clothes. On extended trips, taking a lightweight padded folding chair can add to your comfort level.

When selecting a campsite, remember the three W's: water, wood, and widow makers. You do need to have a water source nearby, but if you are taking a stove, you don't necessarily need a wood source.

CAMPING

However, you will definitely need to choose a site that doesn't have dead trees (widow makers) that could fall on your tent.

Is your site exposed to wind that may whip down the mountain in the evening? Or is it sheltered by some live trees? Is it in a hollow or dry riverbed that could flood in the event of a storm? Change from big boots into soft footwear as soon as you are in camp to protect the camp area as much as you can (as well as your feet).

Erect your food bag lines (unless you have animal-proofed containers) as soon as your tent is up. Erecting food bag lines so that the bags are 15 feet high is not easy. It requires throwing a rock in a bag attached to a light line over two different high limbs and attaching separate ropes and carabiners to butterfly knots that will hang down from the main horizontal rope to be used as Z-drags to hoist the bags.

The horizontal line is then tensioned by trucker's hitches. Sound complicated? It is, so learn how to do it with an expert and practice it before you go. Once set up, it does enable you to easily retrieve and rehoist your food.

Select a "kitchen area" away from your tent. Either bag any waste and take it out or dig a small sump hole for gray water from cooking and washing up that needs to be filled in each night to decrease odors that will attract animals. You should "triangulate" your tent site, kitchen site, and food storage site so they are not close to each other. In bear country, 100 yards between each is optimal.

If this is not possible, do the best you can, but your tent should at least be uphill of the other sites so that the downhill breeze in the evening doesn't carry smells from the food bags or kitchens through the camping area. If you are camping on snow, you can carve out a kitchen with seats and cooking platforms made of snow.

Decide before you go, depending on the area, whether to take WAG Bags to enable you to carry out your solid human waste or whether to take a trowel to help you to dig cat holes for this. Burying toilet paper in wet environments is acceptable (to most people), but do not burn it unless it is in snow, as you could set fire to the duff (dead pine needles) and not even realize you have done that. An hour or so later, the fire you started underground may erupt and set off a whole forest fire. Most people now regard social campfires as unnecessary. If you do make a fire, stick to using existing fire rings or a fire pan. Only downfallen wood should be used, as breaking off tree branches for firewood denudes the area and makes it look terrible for everyone else.

Camping in winter requires a host of other skills that you must acquire through special training. It also involves using heavier clothing and gear, different types of gloves, being able to light stoves with gloves on, and wearing insulated booties or possibly even overboots, felt-lined boots, or double boots. Other necessary skills include knowing how to build an igloo from compressed snow blocks cut with a snow saw or a quinzhee shelter made by making a pile of snow; compressing it with some skis, shovels, or snowshoes; and then hollowing it out. Both types of shelters are warmer than tents once you are inside them.

**Camping in winter requires
a host of other skills that you
must acquire through special training.**

COOKING

Cooking requires either a fire or a stove. Most people take stoves today, as they are cleaner, and you don't have to worry about finding fuel. Different stoves burn different kinds of fuel, such as white gas, denatured alcohol (or methanol), or butane (as in cartridge-type gas stoves). All have different advantages. White gas stoves can be powerful but tend to be very loud; alcohol stoves are slower, but they are quiet and have no moving parts to break; and with cartridge stoves, you simply screw it together and turn it on, but then you need to dispose of the used cartridges. Some stoves use wood. Lighting a camp stove can be dangerous if you don't know what you are doing. Some stoves in the past were called "bivvy bombs" (bivvies are small tents or shelters).

Mistakes include lighting a stove that is placed between your outstretched legs when you are sitting on the ground, thus allowing highly flammable

BIVVY BOMB

substances to be close to your "family jewels"; not tightening cartridges enough and allowing gas to escape and light; spilling fuel that ignites when you light the stove; and refilling a crucible with alcohol when it is not finished burning (the flame often is invisible).

Having learned how to safely light a stove and having practiced before your trip, you could also practice outdoor cooking. The "in the bag" type of dehydrated food is the simplest, as you simply rip the top of the bag, take out the moisture-absorbing capsule, pour in boiling water, leave it for a set time, and then eat it. Many dual-serving packages are sufficient for only one person.

If you are doing the total food planning routine and cooking pancakes, pasta, rice, and so on, you will need a good spice kit that suits your taste as well as some cooking oil. We repack all the ingredients that we take in polythene bags before we go so that we don't carry the weight of extra packaging. Finding everything you need and sorting it before you begin cooking is a good idea. Taking self-rising flour can help you make frybread by mixing the flour, water, and milk powder with some spices to create a dough you can then fry. This basic mix can also be made into pancakes, bread, doughnuts (if sprinkled with sugar), cheese balls, cinnamon rolls, pizza (with added tomato paste, cheese, and pepperoni), or dumplings to be added to stews made with bouillon and, say, noodles. Once you get inspired, your meals become a highlight of the day.

If you are canoe camping, you could take some canned food to enhance this as well. For lots of recipes, consult *NOLS Cookery*, a cookbook put together by the National Outdoor Leadership School.[2] Another caution on oil bottles: always screw the top back on immediately after you have used it. We had an incident where on the second day of an eight-day trip, the two PhDs on the trip came to us for extra oil, having lost all of theirs when it tipped over. They had to beg a little from all the small cook groups to see them through the remaining six days. It is easy to knock a bottle over when camp cooking, but it is also easy to make sure that you screw the top on each time when you need it for cooking.

NAVIGATING

Any electronic device can fail and run out of power.

Navigation requires far more skill development than just taking a GPS unit. A GPS unit can be useful in pinpointing where you are, but, unlike in a car where it tells you blow by blow where to go on roads, when you are on and off the trail in the wild outdoors, you will often have to figure this out using a map and compass. After all, a direct line between waypoints can lead over cliffs and rivers. Also, any electronic device can fail and run out of power. Available apps, such as All Trails, are very useful and can be used on a cell phone; such apps show many trails and also pinpoint where you are—as long as your cell phone works.

So training and practice with a map and compass are essential. When navigating, you should always know whether you are ascending, descending, or on the flat by looking at the map contours. If you are descending but the map indicates you should be ascending, you may not be where you think you are. At any trail junction, you should check the direction of the trails with your compass. At all times, you should be looking at the map and following where you are in relation to the topography, such as a nearby cliff, stream, saddle, or valley. This is a classic "be in the moment" type of situation. If you have worked out a trip plan, staying "in the moment" is easier. The trip plan should be detailed, such as "Half a mile on the trail, going north and ascending to a right-angled bend heading east at grid reference . . ." and so on. Calculate the actual miles as well as the energy miles as described in the "Hiking" section

NAVIGATING

above. Careful preparation of the intended route before you go will keep you on the right track.

Sometimes you may venture off trail. This is rarely a shortcut, as off trail means taking repeated bearings as accurately as possible and following the bearings while heading toward specific targets, such as a rock, tree, or person in the mist or in the dark (with a flashlight). Extra bearings may have to be taken to do doglegs around obstacles, such as rhododendron bushes. Doglegs are done when you cannot get through an obstacle, such as a bog or lake, so you have to head at right angles to where you were going until you have reached the edge of the obstacle, go back on the original bearing until you are past the obstacle, and then go 90 degrees back so you are on the original bearing. If you can see something (say, a specific tree), then it is easy. If not, then you need to measure the distances by pacing or by using a pedometer. You may have to negotiate lots of downfall, cliffs, waterfalls, or streams. One technique is "aiming off" to prevent missing a target by aiming, say, south of it where there is a feature, such as a stream, that could then be followed north. This is used because walking on a dead-accurate bearing is difficult in jungle-like terrain. Remember that going off trail is usually a lot slower than staying on a trail and that navigation requires a lot of practice.

**Training and practice with
a map and compass are essential.**

CANOEING AND KAYAKING

Many drownings while canoeing and kayaking are caused by poor judgment, and most occur when the paddler isn't wearing a lifejacket. Canoeing and kayaking skills, which have a lot of similarities, help you propel the craft forward, backward, or sideways as well as turn or roll back up from being upside down. You need different types of boats to relax and fish (something stable), to go fast (something long and tippy), or to do something in between (large enough to carry gear if you are camping). The main skill for being in open water is to be able to keep going straight, which can often be made difficult by the wind. Wind can make it impossible to canoe and very difficult to kayak, but some kayaks have rudders to assist with this. Another important skill is to be able to rescue each other if there is a capsize far from shore. Not being able to self-rescue might require a very long swim, and not being able to do it quickly

SELF RESCUE

might mean that people get hypothermia from being in cold water for too long. Being able to self-rescue by doing a kayak roll is a huge advantage.

Being able to exit from a capsized kayak is essential and should be practiced with someone else standing next to the boat to assist if needed. Canoes can also be rolled up, but this is almost impossible with a fully loaded canoe if you are canoe camping. It is also necessary to learn how to rescue an exited kayaker or canoeist.

The skills you need change when you go from open water to the river, as a rapid river contains fast chutes, rocks, eddies, holes (recirculating waves), waves, strainers (trees and such obstacles), undercut rocks, cliffs, and sieves (where the water goes through but you can't). Additional techniques needed for white-water paddling consist of maneuvers to get in and out of eddies, through holes, and around and over rocks and to avoid rocks, undercuts, strainers, and some holes.

The initial safety skill for a kayak is practicing a wet exit, which means getting out of the capsized boat by releasing the spray skirt and then leaning forward to "roll forward" out of the cockpit. You should practice self-rescue on easy water first, where you exit the boat, grab the upstream end of it, and keep hold of your paddle as you swim to shore. If you end up swimming down the rapid, you need to be in a safe swimmer position, lying back with your feet up so that they don't get snagged on the bottom in a foot entrapment. Foot entrapments are a common cause of death on rivers. If you are heading for a strainer, you must change tactics to swim on your front at it and fast so that you can try to get on it rather than be swept under it, where you may get snagged by a branch.

Practicing swimming in swift water is the best way to learn, but you should do it in a controlled situation at a carefully chosen spot overseen by experts. Can you rescue your paddling buddies? Go on a swift water rescue course so that you can learn how to rescue each other. Learning how to roll a boat, kayak, or canoe in white water is much safer than swimming with it in a self-rescue. Usually, you learn how to roll in a pool, then practice it in a lake and then in easy white water. There are different types of boat designs for going down rivers or creeks or playing in river features.

Another aspect of canoeing and kayaking is surfing on the ocean. The size of the surf and the kind of

KAYAK SURFING

waves determine how hazardous the surfing is. Starting on one- to two-foot-high waves is optimal. When
turned sideways, you should lean into the wave to
stay upright. Some waves roll in and are good to
surf, whereas others are caused by a steeply shelving
beach where they build up and crash down. These
"dumper" waves are not suitable for surfing. A serious hazard is collisions, as a kayak can be doing 40
miles per hour down a steep wave. If you are going
to collide with someone, you should capsize, as your
body will act as an anchor. You can roll up afterward.
Not being able to roll in surf is tedious, as you need
to keep emptying your boat. Surfing in a canoe or
kayak should not be done among swimmers because
of the possibility of collisions.

**If caught in a rip current, the
swimmer should head sideways
for a while before heading to shore.**

In surf, a swimmer can be rescued by a kayaker
getting sideways to them, having them hold on to the
boat, and then side surfing in. The swimmer holds
on to the middle section of the kayak and helps the
kayaker lean into the wave. All the water that gets
dumped onto the beach from a wave sometimes fun-
nels back out as a rip current. This can be used to
boat out but can't be swam against. If caught in a
rip current, the swimmer should head sideways for
a while before heading to shore. River boats or specialized surf kayaks can be used for surfing. Other

specialized branches of the sport include kite surfing, windsurfing, and wing surfing—all requiring special kites, boards, and sails.

The ocean has other kinds of hazards if you are sea kayaking. The wind is critical. Can you paddle against it if needed to get back to shore? Tidal currents going up and down the coast at different stages of the tide can also be hard to paddle against, so plan to go with the tide. If there is a fall in the seabed, extra waves, called overfalls, will form and can be very large. Where the tidal current races past a headland, it is called a tidal race and may be difficult to cross, depending on the speed of the current. Much more knowledge and a higher skill level are required when venturing into the open water of the ocean as compared to lakes. The Menai Strait between Anglesey and the mainland of Wales squeezes the ocean in tidal races going at nine knots and over overfalls producing large rapids. These rapids are known as the "swellies" and should be attempted only by experienced paddlers with good rescue skills. I have seen people turn into "nervous nellies" thinking they would be washed out into the Irish Sea if they capsized. The same procedures for rescuing each other on lakes apply, but you may be doing it in very rough conditions with large waves. This, of course, requires practice in real conditions and so should be learned on a course. The course should also teach about other safety aspects, such as always wearing lifejackets and using beacons, whistles, and flares when signaling for help.

CLIMBING AND RAPPELLING

Climbing and rappelling are high risk in that any mistakes could result in serious injury or death. Therefore, equipment is vitally important, as is the ability to use it correctly. Ropes, harnesses, and protection, such as quick draws and camming devices, all need to be high quality and in good condition. How old is your rope? How many falls have you taken on it? Have you ever left it on a branch when camping

for critters to nibble on it? Do you know how to correctly buckle your harness, and does the buckle need "locking"? People have died because their harnesses came undone. Do you know how to place "protection" with "running belays" as you lead climb? Does your belayer know how to use the belay device? Can you belay without a device in case you lose it?

Beginning climbing in a climbing gym under supervision is a good idea. Bouldering without ropes but while being spotted by someone can enable you to practice increasingly advanced climbing techniques in a safe manner. Stepping out on a crag should be done initially with experienced climbers and by starting out on easy climbs before tackling harder routes. This can be done on single-pitch climbs that are less than a rope's length before tackling multi-pitch climbs that are far more complicated.

When rappelling, you are totally reliant on your equipment, so not only does your equipment have to be good, but your ability to set the anchor and your technique must be flawless, as you will be leaning back over the drop on your equipment right from the start.

Rock climbing and rappelling are very technical and cannot be learned from a book alone, so be sure to start off under the guidance of a qualified expert.

VIA FERRATA

The via ferrata route is an alternative to rock climbing and mountaineering as participants use fixed ladders and cables to climb. The climber has two leashes from a harness that are attached to safety cables. Routes include ladders, rungs, and bridges. Falls are minimized by the attachment of the climber to safety cables. Routes are graded from easy to extremely difficult. There are many such routes in the European Alps. Equipment includes specialized carabiners and leashes to absorb energy in case of falls. Helmets and harnesses are necessary, and gloves are recommended, as are lights if tunnels are included on the route. Ice axes and crampons might also be required on some routes. You would need to replace your boots with climbing shoes on more difficult rock routes. Injuries do happen, as falls are still possible onto projections, such as rungs and ladders.

MOUNTAINEERING

Much practice is needed, as you have to be able to do an ice axe arrest instinctively.

Mountaineering combines the backpacking, rock climbing, rappelling, and navigation skills discussed above plus additional skills. You may be working on snow and ice, so that's a new set of skills. For general mountaineering, a larger axe is necessary than for vertical ice climbing. Ice climbing is done on steep, vertical overhanging ice with special ice tools (short axes and stiff crampons). In "mixed climbing," one could alternate on a route that involves climbing on snow, rock, and ice. Being able to use an axe for belays and self-arrests requires practice in "safe" conditions where there are good runouts in case you fail. Guidance is needed, as you can easily stab yourself or injure a shoulder if you do it incorrectly. You need to practice falling headfirst, feetfirst, on your back, and on your front. Much practice is needed to be able to do an arrest instinctively.

You also need the skill set of being able to belay using an ice axe or "dead men" (metal plates also known as "dead boys") that you bury as anchors or snow stakes that you have to bury at the correct angle. You also need the skills to travel while roped together on snow. This can be very dangerous, as the assumption that one person falling on a steep slope can be held by the others has been proven many times to be false; falling climbers can slingshot each other down the mountain. A safer way is to use Petzoldt's Sliding Middleman snow technique, where teams of three travel while still anchored by ice axes.[3] It is not as fast as simply climbing roped together, but it is faster than static belay systems.

Yet other skills are necessary if venturing onto a glacier, where you would be climbing roped together in teams of three, so that if the front person falls into a crevasse, the second can hold that person while the third person aids in setting up an anchor to help with the extrication of the front person. The person in the crevasse has to then climb the rope with some kind of Prusik (a knot used to attach a loop of cord around a rope) but can be aided by the others using a loop of the climbing rope as in the Canadian drop loop system.[4] The loop of rope is used to help haul a climber out of the crevasse. Using crampons is an additional skill given that on mixed climbs, you often leave the crampons attached to your boots to climb the rock as well as ice.

Navigation becomes more complicated, as one needs to understand where crevasses are more likely to be, including large ones called bergschrunds, where the ice is pulling away from the head of the glacier, or where there might be "dry" moats, where the glacier melts next to a head wall. As you climb onto the rock face, navigation can't be done from a regular map—you will also need a guidebook detailing the various routes up the mountain. Add in the hazards described earlier regarding ice, falling rock, crossing talus (boulder fields), crossing the other kind of moats (waterfalls and rivers under the snow), soft snow in the late afternoons, or hard snow in the mornings. Being able to move quickly is important so that you are not at or near the summit when the afternoon lightning starts to hit.

Communicating while climbing is done using a series of set calls, such as "on belay," "climbing," and "climb." There are different systems of calls—you need to make sure you are using the same one as your climbing partners. Climbing routes are graded by difficulty, and different systems are used in different countries. Mountain routes are graded differently from rock routes, and if you use gear to climb (aid climbing), it is different again. The systems become meaningful only after you have used them. A "diff" climb in the United Kingdom would be termed "difficult" and in the United States would be termed a "5.6." You can assess what these ratings mean only after you have done some to compare, for example, how much harder a 5.9 climb is than a 5.6. Once you get an understanding, you can be careful about not setting off on a climb that is above what you are comfortable doing.

On the way in and on the way out, rivers might have to be crossed. Crossing a river is a dangerous activity, as once the depth is above your knees, you can easily be swept away.

FAILED RIVER CROSSING

Crossing by linking arms in a line or making a triangle in groups of three where you can support each other can help. You should take a shoulder out of a strap on your backpack or loosen the straps and undo the chest and waist buckles to be able to remove your backpack if you are swept into the water. If you use a rope, the hazards can increase, as, if you lose your footing and are swept downriver until the rope holds you, you can also be pulled under. Using ropes with river crossing is possible but needs special training. We once had to cross the Poudre River in Colorado with a group and luckily had a very tall guy with us. We sent him across with three ropes attached to a release belt (one held him from upstream, one was way downstream so that he could be pulled in downstream if he got swept away, and the third was for later). Once across, he anchored the ropes to a large tree, and we tensioned two of them and got everyone and their backpacks across on what is called a Tyrolean traverse. Halfway through, the ropes were adjusted so that the knot tying the ropes together was on the bank we set off from on the upstream side of the tree, and the ropes were tensioned with a Z-drag system on the other side. The third rope helped to haul people (hanging from their harnesses) and gear across the system. After everyone and their gear were across, the tension was released, the Z-drag system was dismantled, and the rope was pulled across so that we didn't have to leave any gear behind. Sound complicated? It was, but we had practiced it beforehand, and it took approximately four hours, but it was safer than trying to get everyone across by wading.

As you can see, there is a lot of information to know and many skills that need lots of practice for mountaineering. Starting out with getting some backpacking skills is the first thing, then taking a course on mountaineering with a respected organization should be next. Going alone is very unsafe, as something as simple as a twisted ankle could be the end of you. Going with qualified and experienced mountaineers can increase your judgment skills as you progress in different future ascents.

Going alone is very unsafe,
as something as simple as a
twisted ankle could be the end of you.

CAVING

> *As you have only the time
> that you have light from flashlights
> and headlamps, getting lost can
> be a very serious problem.*

Caving offers adventure from the sense of the unknown where cavers venture into dark and sometimes forbidding-looking caves and potholes. Similar to classifications in climbing and river running, caves have very different levels of difficulty. Finding routes can be difficult in complex systems, so most often people go with someone who knows the way. Printed guides and cave surveys are available, but as you progress up and down as well as forward, a complex cave system can become befuddling. As you have only the time that you have light from flashlights and headlamps, getting lost can be a very serious problem. The way forward in a cave can involve walking, scrambling, crawling, squeezing, swimming, rock climbing, rappelling, and ascending ropes and ladders. The skills needed, then, are varied. To begin with, an easy cave with just some walking and scrambling would be a good start, but this is often via a streambed and may involve scrambling up easy sections where water may be flowing, creating stair step–like waterfalls. How deep will the water get? Will you have to swim? What if the roof comes down to the water level? This is a more advanced caving issue that requires holding your breath and ducking under what is aptly called a "duck."

What if the length of the section underwater is longer? Then you are negotiating what is called a "sump." Are you swimming through the sump or crawling through a low tunnel in the sump holding your breath? Both are possible and scary situations, as you will probably also be dragging gear, such as ropes and ladders plus a bag of safety gear, food, and water. Sometimes, the tunnel may require that you crawl in water but still have to breathe. One such place in Yorkshire, England, is known as Hydrophobia Passage. Here, you would be worried if the water did rise, perhaps due to an unexpected thunderstorm outside. You would know if a passage could flood to the roof if there were a lack of formations, such as stalactites, and leaves and debris on the ceiling.

Another necessary skill is the ability to squeeze through tight places that may require exhaling to get through. As you go through, you will probably be thinking, "Can I get back if I need to?" Is the squeeze

CAVING DECISION

horizontal, or is it vertical, such as Hardy's Horror in Dowbergill Passage, another Yorkshire cave? Below the Hardy's Horror squeeze, the passage opens to a bell shape, so you grab onto a small stalagmite to stop plunging 20 feet down. If you follow a lot of squeezes down, then remember that going back out the same way will entail a lot more energy when going back up.

Going down can involve an easy slide down a rift passage (vertical crack) while monitoring the speed by wedging your shoulders. Climbing the same crack requires wedging your back on one side and knees on the other and "thrutching" upward, also called "chimneying." If the drop is not a tight rift but instead a very wide pothole or cliff, then usually a rope is used to rappel, or an electron ladder is used to climb down. Rappelling was addressed in the "Climbing and Rappelling" section, but in caving, ascenders are often already affixed to your chest and seat harness in case you need to ascend back up the rope. The takeoff on the rappel is different in that you can't do the standard lean back because of rope protectors being where the rope will run on the rock. This means that you attach the descender below the rope protectors, sit on the edge, and then swing down.

Ascending can be by ladder or rope. If you're using a ladder, a safety rope is usually used for going both up and down. Others can help the top belayer by hauling someone if they have run out of strength on the ladder. Climbing a metal electron ladder is another skill, as you need to place your hands behind the ladder to grip the rungs to keep the body as vertical as possible, and the objective is to climb quickly. The longer you are on the ladder, the more your strength runs out. Climbing a rope with Prusik devices allows for more rest, as you can sit in your harness that is attached to the rope by the Prusik device. You also have a second Prusik device above you with a handle, so as you step up on a loop attached to it, you push the handle up and then sit back on your other Prusik. It is a skill that requires practice aboveground, as initially you will use lots of excess energy trying to master the technique. But once you do, it is a very efficient way of ascending. Of course, as in climbing and rappelling, this also requires knowledge and skill in setting up belay and anchor systems to anchor the ropes and ladders, including traverse lines that may need to go sideways when getting on and off these vertical pitches.

Some caves at high altitude have ice in them. An example is the Ice Cave in the Tetons. The initial "river passage" is ice, and not far in is an icefall, so you need to attach crampons (metal spikes) to your boots. Not far below this is a second ice fall. There is a plaque at the entrance to the cave warning that it requires "mountaineering techniques," but unaware beginners could easily start walking down the gentle ice floor and end up falling over the drops. Eventually, the ice disappears, but it is a complex route to exit at the Wind Cave, which requires negotiating a pit by using a rope you dropped down the day before. So, all in all, this is an example of, to be safe, needing to go with someone who knows the way and acquiring the skills before trying to tackle such an advanced cave.

Besides the skills you need to move through the cave, you also need to know what safety gear to take and how much food and water you will need. If you run out of batteries or if your lights fail, it will be pitch black such that you can't really move. If you run out of energy, you will also be stuck. There are also the hazards of getting lost or injured. Cave rescues are serious events, although professional teams do provide this service. However, if no one knows where you are, then no one can call for a rescue team. Therefore, it is essential that you inform someone of your plans. Start with easy caves, go on instructional courses to learn the techniques, and go with others who are experienced cavers who know what they are doing.

GORGE WALKING/CANYONEERING

Gorge walking, or canyoneering, is basically the same as caving except that you don't need a light. The physical features are similar to caves—you would be negotiating the gorge by a riverbed, wading and swimming and possibly using some rappels. It could be a rocky gorge streambed through the woods, such as in the Lake District or Yorkshire in England, or more advanced examples in the European Alps. In How Stean Gorge in Yorkshire, you start off sliding over a small waterfall into a pool, then swim on down, hike the limestone riverbed, and slide down chutes while swimming through more pools on the way. You would typically use lifejackets, helmets, and wet suits. In desert regions, such as the U.S. Southwest, the canyons are drier, and the experience is hotter. In both cases, you should take care regarding river heights, as the gorge at normal levels can be fun but at flood levels can be dangerous. Flash floods can change the experience in minutes. Several people were swept to their deaths in a flash flood near Interlaken, Switzerland, in 1999. This event was unusual, but flash floods can happen on regular rivers and in desert areas. Remember that swimming in rivers has the additional potential hazards of foot entrapments, strainers, and hypothermia from cold water.

COASTEERING

Coasteering is another variation of a climbing/swimming adventure pursuit. It started in Pembrokeshire, Wales, and involves traversing a section of coastline by climbing, swimming, jumping, and diving. Ropes and boats are not used, but the equipment is the same as that used in gorge walking: helmets, wet suits, lifejackets, and shoes. Hazards could include impacts with rocks, where ocean waves carry you onto barnacle-encrusted rocks, and hypothermia and drowning are possible.

SEATREKKING

Seatrekking also involves exploring shorelines of seas, lakes, and rivers without the aid of boats, so it involves swimming, snorkeling, free diving, and hiking. Coasteering is usually a four- to five-hour experience, whereas seatrekking can include overnights and longer distances. Additional equipment needed includes a large dry bag that can be towed for camping and snorkeling equipment. The hazards are the same as those of coasteering.

SKIING, SNOWBOARDING, AND SNOWSHOEING

The skills needed for skiing, snowboarding, and snowshoeing are quite different. Snowshoeing is generally done on either flat or gently sloping terrain. Trying to ascend or descend steep slopes using snowshoes is very difficult, and descending steep slopes can result in flips and somersaults. Snowshoes are useful in enabling travel across deep, powdery snow and so are also used in mountaineering approaches until the terrain gets to be too steep. Carrying a heavy backpack for either winter camping or mountaineering can be exhausting without using snowshoes in deep snow, as one can sink two feet or more and end up wading. Even with snowshoes, a group can follow in a line so that less effort is required for people in the back of the line and they can trade leading when the trailbreaker gets tired. The work should not be so hard that it produces sweat, as this becomes a danger when you stop, as the subsequent chilling effect could produce hypothermia.

This technique can also be used for cross-country skiing. Balance is more important with skis, as when you have a large pack, it can be a lot easier to fall.

An alternative to carrying a large pack is to pull a small sled called a pulk sled. Cross-country skis don't attach at the heel, so you can slide forward easily while lifting your heels.

CROSS COUNTRY DAY TRIPPERS

Skis either might have fish scale–type patterns under the foot area where you press down to push back, or you need to apply "sticky" wax there. The remainder of the bottoms of skis need another kind of wax to enable them to glide. Breaking trail with skis is hard work, so switching the trailbreaker often is important. Once in camp, you may have to erect your tent and get around the camping area until you have worked out where you want to dig trails from kitchen, camping, and toilet areas, all while wearing your skis, which can be cumbersome. In Yellowstone, where it was particularly cold, we used to construct either an igloo or a quinzhee hut. The quinzhee hut is constructed by shoveling a large pile of snow, then tamping it down with skis or snowshoes and shovels, letting it "set up," and then hollowing it out to make a snow cave big enough for two to four people. A small, raised sleeping area should be formed so that the cold air drops into a small pit area immediately by the door. A small ventilation hole should be poked through the roof. The temperature inside can rise to a comfortable 32°F or warmer compared to, say, –20°F outside. An igloo requires more skill, as you need to first stomp an area of snow and let it set up, then cut it into angled blocks with a snow saw. The blocks are then used to build a dome. The time to practice this is not when you really need it—the time to practice is in advance.

If your feet do get cold, it is imperative that you speak up so that you can stop and warm your feet.

While in camp, you would likely wear down or imitation down booties, perhaps with overboots as well. While skiing, you have less insulation than you would with boots on snowshoes, so you need to be careful about getting cold feet. Insulated boots and additional insulation that you can strap over your ski boots can help. If your feet do get cold, then it is imperative that you speak up so that you can stop and warm your feet (potentially on someone's belly). If your feet get so cold that you cannot feel them anymore, then you are dealing with possible frostbite, which is serious. Of course, that's why you should have serious cold-weather clothing and equipment.

While you can build a snow kitchen to make cooking easier, you will have to develop the skills to cook and light stoves with gloves on. The fuel in the stove will be the same temperature as outside, so touching it with bare skin could freeze your skin.

Skiing in Yellowstone requires advanced skills to venture away from base camp and climb some mountains. Descending this kind of terrain requires negotiating different kinds of snow and skiing open slopes without tracks so that, for example, you don't break through a hard crust and fall. Turns on this type of terrain require more advanced techniques, such as "Telemark" turns. Mountaineering skis and bindings are available that enable mountaineers to cope with difficult terrain, as the bindings are hinged and allow the heel to be unlocked for traveling on the flat or uphill and then can be locked for descending, where the technique is more like downhill skiing. Skins can be attached to the skis to give more friction for ascending. Ski mountaineering brings with it all the hazards of mountaineering but also the potential for avalanches. You need to be able to recognize avalanche-prone areas and to test slope stability by digging a pit to check snow layers, and you need to carry avalanche rescue equipment, such as transceivers (beacons), shovels, airbag packs, and probes. Concern should also be shown for animals, such as elk, so as not to disturb their grazing on what little food is available to them in winter.

This brings us to downhill skiing, most likely done at a ski resort. Trails are graded in difficulty, so beginners should start on green trails after having some instruction on an easy slope. In the United States, difficulty levels progress from blue to black to double-black diamonds in advancing difficulty. In Europe, the grading system is green to blue to red to black circles in advancing difficulty. The more difficult slopes are steeper, can have moguls (humps in the snow), and carry a higher risk of injury.

Downhill skiing is not intuitive, as you need to turn your body to face downhill as you turn and lean downhill. The steeper the hill gets, the more you lean downhill (tell that to a beginner!). So the early progressions need to be learned in a class so that you don't develop bad habits. This applies to snowboarding as well. Many snowboarders and some skiers often get too brave too soon—before they have sufficient control and think that wiping out is part of the deal. Falling is part of the deal but not because of reckless speed causing you to hit other people or a tree, rock, or vehicle. Skiing or boarding in control is safer for everyone. Most people wear helmets, but don't let that give you a false sense of security—if you hit a tree at speed with your helmeted head, it may cushion the blow to your head some, but it won't protect your neck at all.

Another safety issue is to stay in bounds—don't duck under roped-off areas that the ski resort has deemed unsafe, as you may end up in an avalanche. The resort's ski patrol assesses the slopes and determines their safety, so don't ignore these assessments.

One other safety issue is getting stuck headfirst in a tree well. These are depressions that form around trees, and if you fall headfirst into one, you may become stuck and unable to reach your bindings to release your board or skis. In this event, you may suffocate quickly, or, if you can breathe, you may succumb to hypothermia if no one saw you disappear.

OFF PISTE

If you are skiing off trail where there are tree wells or other hazards, such as cliffs, going alone is not recommended.

Snowshoeing, cross-country skiing, ski mountaineering, downhill skiing, and snowboarding all require different skill sets that are best learned from an instructor. Ski resorts offer lessons and rent equipment. If you want to venture into any of these sports, save yourself a lot of trouble by getting some lessons first. For backcountry skiing, remember that you will be in an environment that can be very harsh, as it is cold, and you can expect at some point to be hammered by a winter storm. Are you prepared for that? Have you had sufficient training?

EVACUATIONS, INCLUDING SELF-RESCUE, RESCUE, AND FIRST-RESPONSE TECHNIQUES

It takes only a twisted ankle to turn an outing into an evacuation. If you are on your own, this is a serious situation. If you are more grievously injured, say, with a broken leg, then without help, you are in jeopardy and will need a rescue team to search for you. Do you have a way to contact someone, such as with a cell phone or satellite phone? Have you designated anyone to take such a call? Have you informed anyone of where you are going?

It takes only a twisted ankle to turn an outing into an evacuation.

If you are with a group and need an evacuation, the decision would need to be made whether to have the group evacuate or call for outside help, depending on the severity of the injury and the difficulty of extrication. The rescue could be a litter fashioned with poles and backpacks, a professional rescue with a Stokes litter (metal or plastic basket) or horse, or a helicopter. Self-rescue by the group requires that the group has practiced making a litter and practiced carrying it, which is no small feat and can be strenuous. And, of course, there may be an injury to deal with before the evacuation. Remember that most evacuations are very long and very painful and can be very expensive.

Dealing with sickness or injuries, such as cuts, torn ligaments, strained muscles, sprained ankles, broken bones, and so on, requires a good first-aid kit and knowledge of how to use it. Wilderness first-aid certification courses are strongly recommended as a prerequisite for outdoor activities, including Wilderness First Aid, Wilderness First Responder, and Wilderness EMT. Examples of reasons for needing first-aid training include someone getting an infected toe because of stabbing a toe on a twig while wearing open-toed shoes or someone getting sick by drinking untreated water or not washing their hands after going to the toilet. Infection is a serious problem in the woods, so wounds should be kept clean, and sharing water bottles is discouraged. Other injuries, such as broken legs, require more specialist skills, such as splinting using equipment already being carried (e.g., foam pads). When should you move a patient, and when should you not? How can you move a patient safely? All these things are taught in the first-aid courses mentioned earlier.

Other courses to consider taking are rescue courses for the type of activity you are doing. If you are rock climbing, do you know how to lower someone from the cliff to a safer ledge? If caving, what can you do with a broken leg? Caving, probably more than most activities, requires a specialized rescue team. Canoeing and kayaking rescues often require fast action, as someone becoming pinned or clinging to a rock on a rapid river will require instant assistance. Are you carrying rescue gear in your boats, including ropes, webbing, carabiners, and Prusik loops to enable a Z-drag or a Tyrolean traverse, to make a rescue? We experienced someone getting stuck in a hydraulic on the River Inn in Switzerland, and guess who had the rescue gear? The guy in the hydraulic had it in his boat, which was headed on its way downriver, so we had to improvise with a chain of lifejackets, and we were lucky enough that the victim was close to shore. Everyone should be carrying rescue gear and know how to use it. You can help put the odds in your favor by setting up a rescue person on a tricky rapid to stand ready to throw a rope if needed. Can you throw it properly and accurately? It takes practice, so your real rescue throw shouldn't be a practice throw. All boaters should attend swift water rescue courses, as river rescues usually have to be done instantaneously. Waiting for external help could be too late.

In summary, emergencies might require first-aid and rescue skills. You owe it to your companions to acquire these skills in addition to those needed for the activity. The information given in this chapter is just the bare bones. You need to research in detail whatever activity you choose to do and preferably take a course to learn how to do it properly.

Remember:
1. Use good judgment.
2. Be here now.
3. Everything takes a lot longer than you think.
4. Look at the Las Vegas odds of bad consequences.
5. Know what you know and know what you don't know.

Control Plans

What "control plans" do you need to enable safer and more comfortable experiences in the wild outdoors? Having read the preceding chapters, you know that many hazards exist in the wild outdoors. Some advice has been given to avoiding these hazards and getting into survival situations, but what else can you do?

In chapter 1, we discuss some mind-sets that can help prevent survival situations. These are "must-knows" and "good judgment." The five things to consider for keeping you safe are as follows:

1. Use good judgment—from Petzoldt.
2. Be here now—from Gonzales.
3. Everything takes a lot longer than you think—from Gonzales.
4. Look at the Las Vegas odds of bad consequences—from Petzoldt.
5. Know what you know and know what you don't know—from Petzoldt.

Petzoldt also came up with the idea of control plans to help avoid getting into survival situations.[1] When I worked with the Wilderness Education Association, we used these on the wilderness courses that we used to teach. Control plans enable you to have safer and more comfortable experiences in the wild outdoors. Petzoldt suggested the following categories of control plans: climate, time, energy, and health.

CLIMATE CONTROL PLAN

Personal climate control can prevent environmental injuries:

• Control its effects—use quality sleeping bags, tents, and clothing (use layering).

• Check the weather before you go.

• Check the coldest and warmest expected temperatures and wind-chill factors.

• Maintain body temperature at around 98.6°F.

TIME CONTROL PLAN

Poor time control can lead to trip failures:

• In groups, synchronize watches so there is no confusion about meeting times.

• Correlate the factors of terrain, distance, altitude, and trail conditions with group expertise and purpose.

• Calculate how much time this group needs to

  ○ travel,

  ○ cook,

  ○ set up camp, and

  ○ get ready for a hike, climb, or paddle.

• Is an "alpine start" (a very early wake-up) necessary?

• Knowledge of the terrain—if you use trails or go off-trail bush pushing. (The difference could be half an hour versus four hours for the same distance.)

• Use "energy miles" in planning (calculate the miles based on energy expended by adding two miles to the miles on the ground for every 1,000 feet of elevation gain).

ENERGY CONTROL PLAN

Overtiredness can lead to accidents:

• Consume food and liquids—use rest stops when hiking every 20, 30, 40, or 60 minutes to provide opportunities for people to fuel up.

• Take good food and eat often; don't skip breakfast.

• Take additives for treating water.

• Do not use "run and stop" techniques—be plodders; don't burn out the weaker members of the group.

• Conserve energy by going steady, keeping a reserve of energy, and eating well.

• Use "energy miles" when planning.

• If you have alpine starts, then take afternoon naps when you can.

• Have rest days on long expeditions.

• Use rest steps and rhythmic breathing for steep terrain and high altitude. (The rest step is where you stop in a position in which you hold your weight on a straight leg so there is less tension in the muscles and is used on steep ground. Rhythmic breathing is where you consciously breathe one breath per step or maybe two or three breaths per step, depending on altitude.)

HEALTH CONTROL PLAN

Common reasons for evacuations on expeditions are poor hygiene resulting in intestinal issues and not preventing or caring for infections in cuts and abrasions:

• Treat or boil water that you drink or use for cooking.

• Always sterilize eating utensils and cups before eating by dipping them into boiling water.

• Always wash your eating utensils and cups with soap as soon as you can after eating, then rinse.

• Always wash your hands after toilet visits.

• Always wash your hands before preparing food.

• Use hand cream regularly to prevent finger ends cracking—especially if you are using antiseptic gels that contain alcohol to clean your hands.

• Use plenty of sunscreen, especially on your nose and ears.

• Do not use drugs except for what is already in your tea, coffee, or hot chocolate (or as prescribed).

- Treat any cuts or blisters immediately.

- Prevent blisters by using good socks, treating hot spots, and applying moleskin to problem spots early.

- Carry a comprehensive first-aid kit and become qualified in Wilderness First Aid.

- Bathe in some way daily—no caveman ethics. Dipping into streams with no soap is okay. Washing with soap and rinsing is good but should be done away from water sources.

- Don't try *not* to poop. Develop a good poop routine that follows Leave No Trace principles (discussed in chapter 7).

- Don't engage in horseplay, as this has been the cause of many accidents.

- Don't take any large knives, axes, or weapons (except bear spray).

- Be careful while handling bear spray and don't damage the cylinder, as this could cause it to leak.

- Don't wear open-toed shoes or Crocs that don't have reinforced soles.

- Don't eat yellow or red snow (caused by urine [yellow] or a type of algae that smells like watermelon [red]).

While you cannot avoid all the hazards in the wild outdoors, you can lower the Las Vegas odds of an accident or injury or survival situation by following Petzoldt's control plans.

Remember:

1. Use good judgment.
2. Be here now.
3. Everything takes a lot longer than you think.
4. Look at the Las Vegas odds of bad consequences.
5. Know what you know and know what you don't know.

Protecting
the Environment

How do we engage in outdoor activities while still protecting people and the environment? This book has focused on how to avoid getting into survival situations to protect anyone who ventures into the wild outdoors. But it is also important to protect the wild outdoors itself.

When we venture out into the wild outdoors, we should know how to treat it with respect. The more we use it, the more damage we do to it, so we should learn techniques to minimize our impact. We want to do as little damage to the environment as we can, whether this be the woods, the mountains, rivers, caves, oceans, or beaches.

LOW-IMPACT TECHNIQUES

When we are camping, we should change into soft shoes in camp, pack out waste, never cut down trees, and use fires only when necessary while using low-impact techniques. Human waste can be buried in cat holes in some environments but in others needs to be packed out using WAG Bags or in cans in fragile or heavily used areas. Generally, in the woods, people should go a distance from the campsite and water sources to dig their cat holes (six to eight inches deep and cover waste with soil). However, on rivers that have large canyons and only a few small campsites, waste needs to be packed out, as another group may camp at the same site, which would be already full of waste. The normal rules for peeing change too, as instead of making sure to urinate away from the stream or river, in a large canyon and big river with limited campsites, one does it in the river.

However, in well-trafficked areas that are dry, such as the Lower Saddle below the Grand Teton where many climbers camp before the summit bid, there might be so much poop that the area becomes smelly and unsanitary. So, both the regulations and the norms require you to pack out waste in a WAG Bag. The Lower Saddle used to have a giant honey bucket that was emptied by helicopter, then returned to an enclosure made of stones. This meant that you were perched high up on a throne when doing your business—not exactly private. But because it was deemed an unnecessary risk for the helicopter pilots, they changed the system to WAG Bags and a more private wooden enclosure. Now the Lower Saddle has two toilet seats, although they're not sectioned off, so social pooing seems to be a Wyoming thing.

Different areas have regulations to enforce packing out waste, such as those in the Lower Canyons of the Rio Grande, but judgment should be used as to whether you pack out your poop in fragile areas regardless of regulations. Another common issue is burning toilet paper. This is a bad idea when you're in the woods, as you could set the duff (the depth of pine needles) alight and not realize it, starting a forest fire that ignites after you have left. Some people recommend using leaves, sticks, stones, or snowballs as alternatives to toilet paper. An exception we have made to burning toilet paper is that, when camping on deep snow, we have burned toilet paper in a hole in the snow to prevent the spring thaw from leaving blobs of paper all around. However, a cautionary tale could help the unwary here. On a course where we had had a lot of recent snow, my co-instructor set himself up with the ritual of pooping in deep snow. Not wanting to use only a snowball, he laid out his toilet paper and lighter, took off his jacket, and dropped his drawers. Unfortunately, he was under a very large fir tree that was loaded with snow.

SNOW-DUMP

As he brushed a branch with the first wipe, the tree decided to unload too, almost burying him. He graciously told us what had happened so that the rest of the group would be more careful about choosing their toilet locations. When one is on a "total food" diet (with lots of grains) and especially for coffee drinkers, when the time comes, the need to go is often fast, so advanced exploration of suitable locations can be helpful.

> *If you are camping in a very dry area with a high danger of fire, then don't make a fire.*

Having mentioned fires, do you really need one? Can you turn the traditional social fire scene into a quiet look at the stars and listen to the night noises of the woods instead? If there isn't a lot of downfall, you shouldn't be breaking off branches or sawing down trees, as this denudes the area and makes it look terrible for everyone else who will visit it later. If a fire is used, then it needs to be contained and put out when you are finished with it by stirring lots of water into it so that no embers remain. If you are camping in a very dry area with a high danger of fire, then don't make a fire.

The other kind of waste that you might have is leftover food, which also needs to be packed out. Alternatively, if you cooked too much, you could eat it for breakfast the next day, but only if it is nonperishable or temperatures are cold. Good planning for the quantity of food you need is necessary to prevent this kind of waste. When cleaning dishes with soap, dispose of the dishwater in a small sump hole away from the camping area that is filled in each evening. If you don't fill it in, the night critters will come scavenging for food bits. If your hole is too shallow, critters will dig it up (this goes for your cat hole too).

Besides waste, simply hanging around a camping area impacts the ground, so a large group creates much more impaction. If you are a larger group, perhaps don't stay for more than one night. Try to choose areas that are less fragile, such as by camping on rock or snow.

Should you camp next to a river or stream? It may be convenient for getting water, but you will affect the wildlife that wants to access it and increase the chances of polluting it. I remember some students who pitched their leftover noodles into a deep pool when we were camping near a river in a deep gorge. We made them free-dive to retrieve the noodles. However, when you are in a gorge and hiking near rivers, the "don't camp next to the river" rule changes, such as it would on the Salmon River in Idaho, where you have no choice, as you are tucked in by the canyon walls. You should also always try to camp away from trails when you can so that you do not obstruct the view of others who are traveling and hoping to see the wilderness, not your outdoor gear.

You may find interesting stuff while outdoors, such as flowers, rocks, and shells. It is best to leave them for other people to see.

Building rock piles that look like pieces of art may appeal to some people but not to those who want

DISRUPTING THE FOODCHAIN

to experience the natural look of the wild outdoors. Scratching names on rocks or trees defaces them. Taking stalactites or other formations from a cave means that they are stuck in a drawer somewhere and that no one else can see them.

The idea of minimum-impact travel and camping led to the creation of the Leave No Trace Center for Outdoor Ethics. The center's Leave No Trace (LNT) approach has been widely accepted by most wilderness-related organizations, especially organizations in the United States that manage public land, such as the U.S. Forest Service, the National Park Service, and the Bureau of Land Management.

LEAVE NO TRACE

The Leave No Trace Center for Outdoor Ethics established the well-known seven principles of LNT. However, the principles are not static, as the center

continually examines, evaluates, and reshapes them.[1]
The seven principles are as follows:

1. Plan ahead and prepare.
2. Travel and camp on durable surfaces.
3. Dispose of waste properly.
4. Leave what you find.
5. Minimize campfire effects.
6. Respect wildlife.
7. Be considerate of other visitors.

The center provides courses and certificates for people wanting in-depth knowledge on how to best protect the environment while still spending time in the wilderness.

Remember:
1. Use good judgment.
2. Be here now.
3. Everything takes a lot longer than you think.
4. Look at the Las Vegas odds of bad consequences.
5. Know what you know and know what you don't know.

Where to Go from Here

You have read about the hazards in the wild outdoors and the things you need to know before you go. Where can you go now to learn how to safely live, travel, and do these activities in the outdoors?

Reading about hazards in the wild outdoors can make you aware of them, but becoming competent in outdoor living skills, travel, and outdoor pursuits requires actual practice. Practicing with peers can be done in places close to civilization, such as doing short hikes and staying at campsites close to a trailhead. Venturing farther afield requires some instruction by taking a course or through a mentor or friends who know what they are doing. Here is some information about going forth into the outdoors.

COURSES

Many organizations teach outdoor living skills, activity skills, travel, and outdoor pursuits, so attending some courses is strongly recommended. Do your research on the organization to see if it is a good fit for you before signing up. Hundreds of organizations teach outdoor pursuits, and so assessing their quality and mission is important. Some countries have accreditation for programs and certificates for leaders and instructors, so this can also help guide your choice. You may want to develop specific activity skills, but the organization you approach may actually be more attuned to tough expeditions for personal development, more general outdoor education, or outdoor leadership. You want to make sure you align your personal goals with the goals of the course.

Just because you're taking a course, you shouldn't let up and forget the five concepts suggested throughout this book:

1. Use good judgment.
2. Be here now.
3. Everything takes a lot longer than you think.
4. Look at the Las Vegas odds of bad consequences.
5. Know what you know and know what you don't know.

Students and guests sometimes think that if they are taking a course, the instructor is "all-seeing" and "all-powerful" and become slack in using their own good judgment. They may do things like stand near the edge of the cliff imagining that their climbing instructor will whip out their cape and swoop down to get them if they fall off. Instructors should do frequent safety briefings before activities start. As mentioned earlier, Paul Petzoldt used to have us do a "Nick the Greek" session in which we brainstormed where Nick the Greek would have bet accidents are most likely to happen when we changed activities. Getting the group involved regularly with safety briefings makes the individuals in the group more responsive to safety issues. In the university courses that we ran, we always gave permission for any student to stop and request a Nick the Greek assessment at any time they felt there was a need.

We also encouraged everyone to be safety aware and to check each other at all times. This may be through checking a knot when climbing or the safety release on a spray skirt when kayaking. Instructors are human, and they do sometimes make mistakes. I have seen an alpine guide forget that he had his ice axe slotted down between his back and backpack (to allow the use of his hands when moving from snow to rock). Just above a long rappel, he took off his backpack, and his ice axe plummeted a couple of thousand feet. Getting down the mountain without an axe was problematic. Another time, at the same spot, a different guide leaned out on a sling (tether) attached to the rock that he had made, but the knot slipped, and he plummeted to the ground. Qualified instructors increase the safety odds but are not infallible. We should always be looking to reduce the Las Vegas odds of an accident, so you and other participants should be constantly looking for safety issues even when you are in a course with expert instructors.

CAMPS

There are many different types of camps. Some are specialized around specific activities, such as canoeing or kayaking. The camp may be like the American summer camp, where participants spend two to five weeks doing a variety of activities in a residential setting where they sleep in cabins. Many of these camps teach outdoor activities. Camp Merrie-Woode in North Carolina, for example, does backpacking, rock climbing, canoeing, and kayaking in addition to activities such as horseback riding, archery, and crafts. They and other camps in the region do serious climbs, such as the "Nose" on Looking Glass Rock, and tackle white water on the Chattooga River. Merrie-Woode campers were paddling the Chattooga long before the *Deliverance* movie made it popular. The youngsters at these camps are often super enthusiastic and learn skills quickly. While working at Merrie-Woode, I remember teaching kayak rolling in the lake early in the morning before breakfast—at the request of campers. Day camps are also a possibility and are often run by private and public recreation agencies.

LOCAL EDUCATION AUTHORITIES

In the United Kingdom, many local education authorities (LEAs) have outdoor centers dedicated to teaching outdoor pursuits. The Whitehall Outdoor Center in Derbyshire was the first in the United Kingdom. I was lucky enough to go there as a 14-year-old and was taught by Joe Brown, who at the time was one of the world's best rock climbers. This stoked my interest in outdoor pursuits and eventually led me to work as an instructor at the Bewerley Park Outdoor Center in North Yorkshire. These places are residential, often in a converted old mansion, a big old house, or even a castle. This is because the weather in the United

Kingdom is so often abysmal that camping the whole time would be very demotivating. The center's students do short expeditions where they camp, but usually after the day's activities, they will go back to the center. Unfortunately, in recent years, the number of these centers still operating has declined. They cater mainly to school-aged students but sometimes hold courses for teachers and the general public. There are national outdoor centers in the United Kingdom, including Plas y Brenin, Plas Menai, and Tollymore. Glen More Lodge is the Scottish national center, and there are other private outdoor centers.

CLUBS

Clubs exist for all activities. Some clubs are more organized than others, and some pay more attention to safety than others. A way to assess quality is to check whether their instructors have certifications. Most club outings are more loosely run than those run by camps, courses, or centers, so you need to be even more aware of safety. But they can be a great way to get out doing an outdoor activity with like-minded people. I started kayaking with the Sheffield Canoe Club back in the 1960s and was well looked after, such as by getting rides to the rivers and the surf because I did not have a car at the time. The club organized quality instruction with a good emphasis on safety. When I went to Australia in 1973, I helped start the Mitta Mitta Canoe Club in North East Victoria to enable boaters to get together for river trips. We drafted several safety rules for club trips and spent many fine days on the rivers. Clubs may have different specializations—in the early 1970s, the Mitta Mitta Canoe Club did long-distance racing, slalom, and white-water racing and paddling. Since the Dartmouth Dam drowned most of the good rapids on the Mitta Mitta River, the club specialized more in long-distance and sprint racing. Clubs exist for other activities as well, such as climbing, caving, and skiing.

GUIDED TRIPS

Guided trips are available for pretty much any type of activity. I have experienced Exum Guides in the Tetons of Wyoming, Mount Cook Alpine Guides in New Zealand, and Yamnuska in Canada for mountaineering but also guided rafting trips on the Main Salmon River and the Middle Fork of the Salmon River. The mountaineering guided trips involved staying in mountain huts, though for some organizations, it is all camping. The group usually prepares the food together in the mountain huts. On the raft-supported river trips, the food is usually prepared by the guides and can be rather high-class food, steaks and all. Wine and beer are often provided as well. The guides on these river trips are usually very accommodating to their guests. It is possible to either sit in an oar raft or paddle a paddle raft, inflatable kayak, regular kayak, or canoe. People often switch around which boats they're using throughout the trip.

Guided trips usually have good staffing ratios, especially for climbing, so there may be only two or three participants per guide. If you want total attention, then you can hire an instructor or guide for one-on-one instruction. This is pricey but can sometimes be well worth it if your goal is to improve technique. Skiing comes to mind here, when as a beginner you may be in a group of 10, often waiting for your turn to be coached. This happened to us in Austria in the 1960s, and we became bored, took off to just try it on our own, and then found that we had picked up a lot of bad habits. So we eventually forked out cash for an instructor to get us back on track.

OTHER ORGANIZATIONS

REI (Recreational Equipment Inc.), although primarily a U.S. outdoor gear store, offers adventure vacations throughout the world. This includes rock climbing, mountain biking, kayaking, backpacking, road biking, photography, and snowshoeing. The Mountaineers is a nonprofit based in Seattle, Washington, that specializes in mountaineering; hosting courses, classes, and social events; and publishing books. The Wilderness Education Association offers individual credentialing and program accreditation. Its courses are run through universities and other organizations. The Appalachian Mountain Club is another nonprofit organization that promotes wilderness protection and enjoyment through education and trips in the eastern United States. Other associations include the Association for Outdoor Recreation and Education, where many members are from university recreation programs and military recreation, and the Association for Experiential Education, which has its roots in Outward Bound.

In the United Kingdom, the Institute for Outdoor Learning provides the latest in outdoor news and information for professionals in the field. Canada has the Outdoor Council of Canada, which promotes the integration of outdoor education and activity into the Canadian identity. Education Outdoors New Zealand supports outdoor education in New Zealand. Outdoor Education Australia represents outdoor educators, teachers, and organizations in Australia.

NATIONAL BODIES

National bodies act as umbrella associations for outdoor industries, training, and education. The following is a small sample:

- Australian Outdoor Council

- Outdoor Council of Canada

- NZOIA (New Zealand)

- Ireland's Association for Adventure Tourism

- English Outdoor Council

- Institute for Outdoor Learning (United Kingdom)

- Outdoor Industry (United States)

- Association for Experiential Education (United States)

- Wilderness Education Association (United States)

- Association of Outdoor Recreation and Education (United States)

National bodies exist for all activities, such as the New Zealand Speleological Society, the British Canoe Union, and the American Canyoneering Association, so search online with terms such as "national association" or "national organization" for whichever activity you want to pursue. The sites will give information on trainings, certifications, technical advice, and workshops.

MAGAZINES, JOURNALS, AND BLOGS

Many magazines cover outdoor activities, gear, techniques, and education. Some examples are *Outside*, *Alpinist*, *Backpacker*, *Climbing*, *Powder*, *The Explorers Journal*, *Canoe and Kayak*, *Kayak Session*, *Paddling Magazine*, *Rock and Ice*, *Skiing*, and *Powder*. Many also include YouTube videos in their articles if you read them online. Indiscriminate viewing of online videos should be done with caution, as anyone can post activity technique videos—they can be as easily useful as full of bad advice.

Blogs include the Big Outside, Moja Gear, Powder Hounds, Modern Hiker, the Adventure Blog, the Adventure Junkies, Uncharted Backpacker, and Young Adventuress. Professional journals written mainly for professional outdoor educators include the *Journal of Outdoor Recreation, Education, and Leadership*, the *Journal of Adventure Education and Outdoor Learning*, the *Journal of Experiential Education*, the *Australian Journal of Outdoor Education*, and the *New Zealand Journal of Outdoor Education*.

BOOKS

Instructional books are available for all activities, as are guidebooks and maps. Some activities, such as rock climbing, require detailed descriptions of routes with associated diagrams. For groups on expeditions, a small portable "library" is useful on the local flora and fauna, history, geology, geomorphology, and geography. Small books have even been designed to put into your first-aid kit. Reading up on the wild outdoors is a good plan, but experiential learning needs to follow. When you are back in your armchair next to the fire, it is also interesting to read classic books about adventurers such as Shackleton, Nansen, Scott, Hillary, Bonington, Habler, Messner, Herzog, Whymper, and others.

COLLEGES AND UNIVERSITIES

Many colleges and universities do programs for outdoor pursuits through their recreation departments, and some have academic degree programs in this area. A few even have graduate programs in outdoor experiential education. College students are likely able to access courses and trips very inexpensively. Many colleges have artificial climbing walls, and, as they usually have swimming pools as well, kayak rolling sessions are often available. I worked for a college program while at Minnesota State University, Mankato and, besides activity workshops on rock climbing, cross-country skiing, and canoeing, we organized ski trips to Yellowstone and backpacking trips to Big Bend, Texas. A similar program at Concordia College went even further with college trips to Europe, including backpacking in Austria, skiing in Norway, and caving and sea kayaking in England. Students even got to ski across Greenland and Lapland. The college you are attending will probably have an outdoor program that offers courses and instruction to varying degrees.

SCOUTING AND THE DUKE OF EDINBURGH'S AWARD SCHEME

I got my start in outdoor pursuits through scouting. As camping and the outdoors have always been a significant part of scouting for boys and girls, it is often a catalyst for many people getting into outdoor activities. Another organization that encourages outdoor pursuits and expeditions is the Duke of Edinburgh's Award Scheme, which is the leading youth achievement award program and is practiced in 144 nations.

BUDDIES/FRIENDS

Do all of your friends carry rescue gear? Do they know how to use it? Have they been on a rescue course?

You will mostly likely go with your friends when engaging in outdoor activities. Take care to look after each other. If you are the newcomer to an activity, ask questions about the difficulty of the climb, cave, or river wherever your friends are taking you. Try to assess if you will be stepping out too far—remember that it's best to build your skills gradually before attempting something difficult. If you are a more experienced member of the group, take care of the less experienced and don't push them to do something above their abilities. The possibility exists of an "epic," which is what we used to call events where bad things escalated, such as several capsizes on a river or ocean at the same time. It could be a caving trip that lasts 12 hours instead of four or a climb where you end up staying the night. Eventually, everyone should develop self-rescue and first-aid skills so that you can help each other out if need be. If you are in canoes or kayaks, everyone should have rescue gear in their boats. If only one person has the rescue gear and that person is in trouble, what do you do? This happened to us on the River Inn in Switzerland in 1972, where someone (who had the rescue gear) got stuck in a hole but fortunately was very near the right bank of the river. Two of us managed to get near to him, but we didn't have a rope and so had

HYDRAULIC RESCUE

to make a chain with our lifejackets to hold onto so that we could reach over a small cliff into the hole. We managed to get him out, minus his boat, which was lost downstream (with the rope). I have always taken a rope and rescue gear ever since. Do all of your friends carry rescue gear? Do they know how to use it? Have they been on a rescue course?

RESCUE AND FIRST AID

Eventually, you will want to gain knowledge and experience in basic rescue and first aid. By far the best way to do this is to take courses. Search and rescue skills are technical skills for all activities, so this needs to be taught by professionals at well-known mountain centers or organizations. If you enjoy this, you can then join a rescue team, which is great service as well as helpful for gaining useful skills for looking after your friends. For skiing, you can join the ski patrol, which has its own organization for rescue, evacuation, and first aid. Other organizations exist for backcountry first aid with different levels of expertise. These are often termed wilderness first aid, wilderness first responder, and wilderness emergency medical technician. The courses are intense and vary in length from a couple of days to two weeks; they include lots of practical experience in dealing with "contrived" incidents. They also include studying lots of medical information. If you gain any of these certificates, you are usually required to recertify every two years.

DISABILITIES

People with disabilities are not excluded from outdoor pursuits. Often, it means that some adaptation needs to be made. Mountaineer Tom Whittaker, for example, put "one foot" forward on Mount Everest back in 1998 when he became the first leg amputee to summit Everest. He started the Wilderness Cooperative Handicapped Outdoor Group at Idaho State University and took disabled students rock climbing, ice climbing, and rafting and then trekking to the Everest Base Camp.

In 1982, I was involved in taking a group of people with disabilities kayaking and canoeing down the Vermillion River in Minnesota. The disabilities included cerebral palsy, paraplegia, quadriplegia, hemiplegia, and sight impairment. The trip was one week long and involved capsize practice, rescue practice, easy rapids, negotiating serious portages, and camping with several wheelchairs. With adaptations, everyone paddled and completed this expedition. Most activities can be adapted. Some ski resorts have adaptive skiing programs. Some organizations specialize in doing adapted activities, such as Wilderness Inquiry in the United States and Motability in the United Kingdom.

ORGANIZATIONS THAT PROTECT THE ENVIRONMENT

Some organizations protect, gain access to, and preserve wild areas, including wilderness, rock climbing sites, caves, and rivers. These include the following organizations:

Worldwide
Greenpeace

World-Wide Fund

United Nations Wildlife Environmental Protection

Wildlife Conservation Society

Sea Shepherd Conservation Society

Friends of Nature

International Rivers

United States
Wilderness Society

Sierra Club

The Nature Conservancy

Natural Resources Defense Council

National Wildlife Federation

Surfrider

Earth Justice

National Parks Conservation

Conservation Fund

American Whitewater

One Percent for the Planet

Wild Foundation

American Rivers

Access Fund (climbing)

Leave No Trace

Canada

Environment Canada

Canadian Parks and Wilderness

Ecojustice Canada

Nature Canada

Sierra Club Canada

Western Canada Wilderness Committee

Ontario Alliance of Climbers

Alpine Club of Canada

Australia

Australian Wildlife Conservancy

Bush Heritage Australia

Nature Conservancy Australia

Tasmanian Land Conservancy

Trust for Nature

Australian Climbing Association

Australian Speleological Federation

New Zealand
Nature Conservancy in New Zealand

Maruia Society

Native Forest Action Council

Ecologic Foundation

NZ Walking Access Commission

ECO—Environment and Conservation Organizations of Aotearoa New Zealand

Ireland
Irish Environmental Network

National Parks and Wildlife Service

Speleological Union of Ireland

Mountaineering Ireland

United Kingdom
British Association of Nature Conservationists

Ramblers Association

Countryside Alliance

British Canoe Union

British Mountaineering Council

Council of Northern Caving Clubs

British Caving Association

We can become involved through an organization that does the heavy lifting legally and politically.

This list is only a sample of organizations working to protect the environment. Besides protecting the environment through low-impact techniques, we can become involved through an organization that does the heavy lifting legally and politically. Besides protecting wild areas from commercial operations and overuse, these organizations also help with gaining access.

In the United States, American Rivers is an example of an organization that ensures open access when agencies such as the U.S. Forest Service close them. A recent example was when American Rivers brought a successful legal challenge to open up the Upper Chattooga, which had been restricted to only hiking and fishing. They also lobbied the local power companies to do releases on dammed rivers, such as the Tuckaseegee. In general, access to rivers is good in the United States unlike in the United Kingdom, which has strict laws biased toward landowners. Only 2 percent of all rivers in England and Wales have public access rights. The British Canoe Union is working on this with the Rivers Access Campaign. Access was gained in the United Kingdom for walkers with the "right to roam," enabling access to mountains, moors, heaths, and downs. I remember being walked off the Nidderdale moors by a gamekeeper with a group of youngsters I was taking hiking in the

1970s. The Ramblers won the right to roam through legal battles and mass trespasses and came into effect in 2005. In New Zealand, conservation groups challenged the government's plans to harvest native forests and replant with an exotic species. This resulted in the Maruia Declaration to phase out the logging of virgin native forests in New Zealand. Almost all of its stipulations were met in the following 30 years.

So to combat the encroachment of extractive commercial activities such as logging, mining, and water activities and to gain access on restricted lands, agencies such as those in the above list need support through memberships and funds to help us all be good stewards of the environment.

GOING ON YOUR OWN

Consequences can be serious for going alone in the wild outdoors, as simply twisting an ankle can

GOING IT ALONE

immobilize you. Many people have disappeared in the Great Smoky Mountains with no trace. What likely happens is that people get lost or don't have enough food, water, or the correct clothing, or perhaps they fall and injure themselves, eventually dying and then becoming bear food when the bears find their decomposing bodies. This happened because they had no one with them to get help and didn't leave information with anyone saying where they were going.

There can be serious consequences for going alone in the wild outdoors.

Well, you might say, "but we have our cell phones!" They may not work where you are going. Their batteries may die. On some expeditions to remote places, you could take satellite phones, but of course they are electronic and need batteries as well. You can bring portable solar panels to charge batteries, but anything electronic could always still fail. Technology may be giving you a false sense of security.

How many people should go together? This depends on the situation. How many people would it take to find you and dig you out of an avalanche in under half an hour? How many people would it take to complete an evacuation if you were to do it yourselves? We practiced this on all our college trips with around 10 people carrying a litter made from backpacks, and we needed everyone switching out to carry someone—and it was still always very difficult.

What about activities such as caving? When we were young and thought we were invincible, four of us, all instructors (but not yet 25 years old), decided to do Dowbergill Passage, an offshoot from Dow Cave in Yorkshire where we would regularly take students. We used to take them past the entrance to Dowbergill while telling the tales of horrific rescues down there. It is a mile long almost dead straight from Dow Cave to the exit, Providence Pot, but it's a tortuous route and vertical maze, so, without a guide, finding your way is extremely difficult. The hazards to negotiate include boulder chokes (boulders stacked on each other), vertical rifts where you can be traversing high up with your back on one wall and knee on the other moving sideways, loose boulders in places, and the "Blasted Crawl," the "Terrible Traverse," and "Hardies Horror" (the vertical tight slot). Many rescues were done at this time in the late 1960s when cavers ran out of lights after getting lost and then succumbed to hypothermia. But, we thought, "it can't be that bad" and decided to do it one evening, not wanting to waste a day (the day after we had planned to go climbing).

The four of us left word with someone in case we didn't get back by morning. It ended up taking twice as long as we thought. We had to throw away our caving suits, which were ripped to shreds, and we had swollen knees, as we had negotiated several high rifts being in the wrong place. In fact, we thought we did the Terrible Traverse about three times before we got to the real one. We didn't go climbing the day after, as we—unsurprisingly—needed time to recover.

A week later, three other instructors decided to do it. Part way in while negotiating a boulder choke, a boulder moved and pinned someone. They decided to have one person stay and the other go for help. An hour later, a light appeared heading back toward the boulder choke—but it was the person going for help who had gotten turned around while heading out. Their spirits must have plummeted at this point. They decided that they would have to leave the pinned person, as it would take two people to find the way back out to the Blasted Crawl, then out of the exit, Providence Pot. A large rescue ensued that was organized by the Upper Wharfedale Fell Rescue Squad and many volunteer cavers. The rescue involved dragging out the injured caver in a neoprene bag on a drag stretcher. Some of the Blasted Crawl roof had to be broken off to get him through. He had to be hospitalized for hypothermia and a shoulder injury. If there had been four cavers, one could have stayed with the trapped person; if there had been only two cavers, perhaps no one would have made it out. Had they told anyone where they were going? Yes, but if they hadn't, then who knows what their chances of survival would have been. The rescue was difficult and exhausting because of the nature of the cave.

The activity, then, determines how many should be in the group. In the above example, a minimum of four was really needed. For a glacier travel, three on a rope is advised so that the middleman can halt the fall of a leader into a crevasse and the third climber can assist in the extrication. For skiing, if you are alone and negotiating trees, no one will be there to help extricate you if you go into a tree well. For alpine climbing, two may be faster than three where speed is really important, but if there is an accident, you would be shorthanded to deal with it. Two rope teams of two would be safer. One person climbing alone means that a fall could be deadly. What about one person heading out into mountainous terrain?

While setting up camp at Skinny Dip Lake in the Tetons one year, we had a lone graduate student walk into our camp. Skinny Dip Lake is a misnomer, as at this time of year (early June), there was eight feet of snow. But later in the year, because the lake is shallow, it is one of the only lakes you can enjoy getting into because it warms up. On this occasion, a lot of snow had fallen, and more was in the forecast. A three-day storm was on the way. We (a group of 12) were there practicing spring mountaineering techniques and outdoor leadership. What was the lone graduate student doing? She was taking tree core samples for her graduate studies. Had she not checked the weather forecast? Did she feel safe on her own? We had just resupplied with a week's worth of food and knew we were in for a storm, so we were hunkered down with snow kitchens, cook tarps, and four-season tents. We invited her to join us and stay until we headed back down. She was anticipating a one overnight stay. It ended up being three overnights before we could move. Her roommate back home called the Forest Service when she didn't return. The Forest Service knew we were in the same spot as she was, as they had our permit itineraries, so they told her roommate that our group knew what we were doing and would look after her. There was no cell service at this time. She wanted to leave immediately after the storm abated, but this required a steep slope descent on new snow (a high risk for an avalanche), so we persuaded her to stay one more day. When we eventually headed out, we crossed some mountain lion tracks. What if she had headed out early and bumped into the mountain lion? What if we hadn't been there to help her through the storm with our extra food? She had left word of where she was going, so that probably would have meant a rescue operation, but it would have been a difficult rescue in the middle of a three-day storm. Everything worked out in this case, but the decision to go alone was not a good one.

SUMMARY

At various levels, most people are able to do some kind of outdoor activity. Learning about what you don't know is the first step, followed by practice under guidance and by practice with others. This can be followed by learning about basic rescue and first aid.

PARTING THOUGHTS

*There are things
to know—before you go.*

Throughout this book, you have learned that bad things can happen to the unwary and that you need to know certain things—before you go. You have learned that venturing into the wild outdoors often requires small steps to learn the skills needed. Those skills are best learned with an instructor on a course or with a guide or with friends who can mentor your progress. We all want to live to be old mountaineers, climbers, kayakers, cavers, skiers, and canoeists, so knowing what you don't know about the wild outdoors can help with that.

The benefits can be lifelong pursuits that keep you healthy and moments that will live forever in your memories—those peak experiences. You will remember your experiences of simply being in the wild outdoors with the wind in your face, the sun on your back, the smells of the sea and the forests with their luxuriant foliage, the grand vistas of the moorlands and deserts, the sense of power emanating from the storms, the ocean waves, and the mighty rivers.

Your journey through life can be enhanced by the numinous experiences gained in the wild outdoors, what Jung would refer to as the archetypal journey. Remember that Roszak, in the epilogue to his book *The Voice of the Earth*, suggested that this is the journey of a lifetime, and "the person is anchored within a greater universal identity." Our identity with the natural world from which we get our enjoyment and personal growth should also be protective for itself and for future generations. A religious view of nature is necessary for this to happen, so enjoy the wild outdoors but invest in it too—in whatever way you can find to do that. Know what you don't know about conservation as well as safety.

*We all want to live to be
old mountaineers, climbers,
kayakers, cavers, and canoeists.*

Remember:
1. Use good judgment.
2. Be here now.
3. Everything takes a lot longer than you think.
4. Look at the Las Vegas odds of bad consequences.
5. Know what you know and know what you don't know.

Acknowledgments

Thanks to Chelsea Phipps for initial critiques and editing, to the late Paul Petzoldt for imparting his wisdom throughout the years, to Diana Veal for the back cover photo, and to Fred Schmidt for the cartoons.

Notes

INTRODUCTION

1. http://www.westerncarolinian.com/news/view.php/417546/WCU-Senior-Injured-at-Area-Waterfall.

2. "Symmetry Spire—A Very Bad Year," *Off Belay*, January–February 1973, 44.

3. "Fall onto Snow, Fall into Moat, Inadequate Equipment, Inexperience," *Accidents in North American Mountaineering* 4, no. 6, issue 36 (1983): 67.

4. https://www.princeton.edu/~oa/safety/hypdeath.shtml.

5. P. K. Petzoldt, *The New Wilderness Handbook* (New York: Norton, 1984).

6. Laurence Gonzales, *Deep Survival: Who Lives, Who Dies, and Why: True Stories of Miraculous Endurance and Sudden Death* (New York: Norton, 2003), 62.

CHAPTER 1

1. "Understanding the Teen Brain," University of Rochester Medical Center Health Encyclopedia, https://www.urmc.rochester.edu/encyclopedia/content.aspx?ContentTypeID=1&ContentID=3051.

2. Maurice L. Phipps, with Stephanie L. Phipps and Chelsea L. Phipps, *Outdoor Instruction: Teaching and Learning Concepts for Outdoor Instructors* (Trenton, GA: BookLocker, 2017).

3. Theodore Roszak, *The Voice of the Earth: An Exploration of Ecopsychology* (New York: Touchstone, 1993), 319.

4. "Adventure—An Inner Journey to the Self: The Psychology of Adventure Expressed in Jungian Terms," reprinted in Phipps, *Outdoor Instruction: Teaching and Learning Concepts for Outdoor Instructors* (Trenton, GA: BookLocker, 2017).

5. Paul Petzoldt, *Teton Tales: And Other Petzoldt Anecdotes* (Merrillville, IN: ICS Books, 1995).

CHAPTER 3

1. "A Year after Daring Rescue, Teton Lightning Incident Reminds of Backcountry Danger," *Casper Star and Tribune*, July 24, 2011, http://trib.com/news/state-and-regional/a-year-after-daring-rescue-teton-lightning-incident-reminds-of/article_b1ca5efa-3d6d-5dc8-822a-e712229323fe.html.

2. "64 Years Later: A Survivor Remembers the Darby Girls Camp Tragedy," *Teton Valley News*, August 13, 2015, https://www.tetonvalleynews.net/news/years-later-a-survivor-remembers-the-darby-girls-camp-tragedy/article_e6ad91d4-4119-11e5-a077-d7a8fd230069.html.

3. "Lake District Walker Suffers from Hypothermia while Walking on Scafell Pike," *Westmoreland Gazette*, October 26, 2014, http://www.thewestmorlandgazette.co.uk/news/11560206.Lake_District_walker_suffers_from_hypothermia_while_walking_on_Scafell_Pike.

4. "John Sandell and Malcolm Buckman," *Monument Australia*, http://monumentaustralia.org.au/themes/people/

tragedy/display/20181-john-sandell-and-malcolm-buck
man.

5. "Mount Hood's Deadliest Disaster," *Outside Online*,
November 2, 2018, https://www.outsideonline.com/235
7451/mount-hood-disaster-1986.

6. Paul Petzoldt, personal communication, 1986.

7. Paul Petzoldt, with Raye Carleson Ringholz, *The New
Wilderness Handbook* (New York: Norton, 1984).

CHAPTER 4

1. Sidney Sullivan, "MAP: Fatal Bear Attacks in North
America," *Alaska's New Source*, July 5, 2017, https://www
.ktuu.com/content/news/MAP-Fatal-Bear-Attacks-in-Nor
th-America-432734333.html.

2. David J. Wesley, "10 More Terrifying Killer Fish,"
Listverse, March 31, 2013, https://listverse.com/2013/
03/31/10-more-terrifying-killer-fish.

3. Gael Fashingbauer Cooper, "Author Revisits How
'Into the Wild' Subject Died in Alaskan Bus," *Today*,
https://www.today.com/popculture/author-revisits-how
-wild-subject-died-alaskan-bus-8C11141443.

CHAPTER 5

1. Paul Petzoldt, *The New Wilderness Handbook* (New
York: Norton, 1984); Maridy McNeff Troy and Maurice
L. Phipps, "The Validity of Petzoldt's Energy Mile Theo-
ry," *Journal of Outdoor Recreation, Education, and Leadership* 2, no. 2 (2010): 245–59.

2. Claudia Pearson, ed., *NOLS Cookery*, 7th ed. (Lanham, MD: Stackpole Books, 2017).

3. Maurice L. Phipps and T. Murdock, "Paul Petzoldt's Sliding Middleman Snow Technique," *Journal of Outdoor Recreation, Education, and Leadership* 6, no. 1 (2014): 68–76.

4. Tom Denshki, "Crevasse Rescue: The Step by Step Instructions," http://www.mountaineersbcs.org/crevasse.html.

CHAPTER 6

1. Paul Petzoldt, *The New Wilderness Handbook* (New York: Norton, 1984), 33.

CHAPTER 7

1. Leave No Trace, "The 7 Principles," https://lnt.org/why/7-principles.

Index

About the Author

Maurice L. Phipps is professor emeritus of parks and recreation management in the Department of Human Services at Western Carolina University. He is on the Presidential Council for the Wilderness Education Association, having been an instructor and board member for 28 years. He apprenticed with legendary mountaineer Paul Petzoldt during his time in the Wilderness Education Association and later cotaught expedition courses with him.

Phipps has written and contributed to 50 different articles and publications and is the author of three other books. He has worked in public, nonprofit, and private agencies for 50 years, including at Iowa State, Cal Poly, the Western State University of Colorado, and Western Carolina University. He has taught in the United States, the United Kingdom, and Australia and gained qualifications through the British Canoe Union (British canoe coach), the Australian Canoe Federation (diploma), and the Wilderness Education Association (instructor). Phipps has also received several teaching awards from Western Carolina University and three service awards from the Wilderness Education Association.